Picture Books *Sans Frontières*

Picture Books *Sans Frontières*

Penni Cotton

Trentham Books

First published in 2000 by Trentham Books Limited

Trentham Books Limited
Westview House
734 London Road
Oakhill
Stoke on Trent
Staffordshire
England ST4 5NP

British Cataloguing in Publication Data
A catalogue record for this book is available from the British Library
ISBN 1 85856 183 3 (hb ISBN 1 85856 184 1)

Cover picture taken from *Une nuit, un chat* by Y. Pommaux by kind permission of the publishers, L'ecole des loiirs, Paris.

Trentham and the author would like to thank the publishers of all the books in the EPBC (listed on p.141) for permission to use illustrations from the books.

Designed and typeset by Trentham Print Design Ltd., Chester and printed in Great Britain by Cromwell Press Ltd., Wiltshire.

Contents

For Oliver

Acknowledgements

Without the help and support of the following colleagues in Europe, this book would not have been possible:

Anna Adamik-Jászó, Maria Pia Alignani, Jacques Beaucamp, Susannah Beer, Yves Beernaert, Bregje Boonstra, Greg Brooks, Philippe Carter, Gràinne Darlington, Gwen Davies, Michel Defourny, Leen Derveaux, Mieke Desmet, Eva Dietriche, Robert Dunbar, René Duriez, Epp Eelmaa, Juan José Lage Fernandez, Frank Flanagan, Geoff Fox, Jean Foucault, Marta Maria Garcia Suarez, Catriona Heffernan, Alan Hill, Ranka Javor, Mogens Jansen, Edith John, Winfred Kaminski, Lena Kåreland, Meni Kanatsouli, Celia Keenan, Liliane Kjellman, Vasiliki Labitsi, Annemie Leysen, Menna Lloyd Williams, Jamie MacAskill, Francis Marcoin, Stuart Marriott, Margaret Meek Spencer, Barbara Mladek, Marina Moriati, Mare Müürsepp, Heidi Niemann, Isabel Nières, Marie-Louise Olofson, Emer O'Sullivan, Jean Perrot, Lilia Ratcheva, Edith Pikous-Ströger, Carla Poesio, Romain Sahr, Igor Saksida, Muhamed Sarajlic, Renate Schellander, Peter Schneck, Karin Sollat, Daniela Stefanescu, Karen Trondhjem, Gella Varnava Skoura, Isabel Vila Maior, Denise Von Stockar, Fraukia Wiersma Depreux, Michael Zajac and all the teachers who used the EPBC in schools.

Chapter One
Bringing a European Dimension
to Primary Education

As we move towards a more integrated Europe all children within the European Community need to develop some awareness and understanding of their European neighbours. There have been edicts from the European Union for some time expressing the need to implement a European dimension in education. There have been suggestions about how this might be done but these have generally been directed towards secondary education. The main concern of *Picture Books Sans Frontières* is primary education, exploring how universal themes in children's literature, particularly the visual narratives of picture books, might cross cultural barriers and thus bring a European dimension to primary classrooms.

Picture Books Sans Frontières introduces readers to the delights and fascination of picture books from the European member states. The visual narratives in these texts have the potential to help children to learn more about their European neighbours and the minimal texts develop linguistic and literary awareness. Studies concerning picture books, particularly those in the UK, have generally tended to concentrate on ways in which the polysemic nature of the texts can enhance children's love of books and facilitate the reading process. The focus of these studies has generally been on picture books produced by British authors and illustrators, with scant attention paid to the excellent material produced in other European countries.

This book focuses on the universal childhood themes which permeate certain texts, and suggests ways in which children throughout Europe might be given the opportunity to empathise with each other and learn about cultural similarities and differences. Through a study of the interaction between visual and auditory stimuli it also aims to identify how children can begin to understand literary forms and gain greater linguistic understanding.

Picture Books Sans Frontières explores a number of theoretically-based practical ways in which educationalists can develop classroom activities to support the upper primary curriculum, while at the same time broadening children's horizons by introducing them to new literary, linguistic and cultural elements. They apply to England's National Literacy Strategy (DfEE, 1998), which requires pupils to have an understanding of literature at word, sentence and text levels but gives limited guidelines about the specific literature to be used.

Chambers (1996: 9) remarks that 'Books are only ink on paper. But more than ink on paper, books are people'. I have always considered books to be my 'friends' but as a teacher and teacher educator I have noted how picture books have become the particular friends of children and teachers, and these certainly include European books.

Working in Europe and arranging student exchanges in a number of European countries has brought me to many primary schools in the European Community. What was apparent everywhere was the immediacy of communication between pupils and trainee teachers evoked by picture books. Sharing picture books became an entrée into the children's world for these student teachers. Spoken language was no longer a barrier – the visual narratives of these well-chosen books and their universality of themes enabled the texts to become a catalyst for communication.

I too enjoyed these shared experiences. In all the countries I visited, young children were to be seen immersed in their picture books. If I showed an interest in what they were reading, the children began to point to the pictures and tell me the story. It was much easier in the countries where I understood their language but even in those where I did not the books facilitated understanding and communication. In Sweden, for example, I was able to draw on my general knowledge of how language works and the structure of stories. But it was the visual narratives to which the children referred when they told these often familiar tales that were crucial to my understanding. Thus I became absorbed not only in the Swedish stories but also in the language and culture of Sweden. I began to reflect on what I was learning personally from this experience.

In Sweden, simultaneously looking at and listening to a new language enabled me to see the similarities between Swedish and other languages, especially my own. Then, with the visuals to reinforce this auditory input plus my own understanding of likely story narratives and language, I noticed that I was approaching these texts in the way that young children first learn to read – using all the visual and auditory clues I could plus a developing sense of how language works. Many of the books were totally unfamiliar in style and content and I began to think that some of these texts which seemed unusual and often offered insights into the culture should be made available to English children. If I had acquired new understanding while sharing these stories with young Europeans then perhaps older primary school children, as well as trainee teachers, could use the books, too. The stories would be not only from other European countries but also in other European languages.

2

In 1993 I attended a conference in Belgium organised by the European Commission, designed to encourage teacher educators to develop materials which would imbue a European dimension in their courses. This allowed me to put forward a tentative suggestion that we use European children's literature to implement a European dimension in primary education. I was encouraged to submit a proposal which would involve specialists in children's literature from all member states of the European Union. After several months of negotiation, finances were made available for a project to investigate the possibilities of using European picture books to help children within the European Community to understand more about each other.

For the project to move forward specialists in children's literature had to meet. So a symposium was organised at which each participant would give a paper relating to children's literature in his/her country and focus on a number of culturally representative picture books which could be used in a proposed European picture book collection. The books would then be analysed and one from each country selected together with a cassette in the original language, written translations into English and practical activities. The materials would be designed for use in upper primary classrooms.

Thus the European Picture Book Collection (EPBC) was created. Originally it was designed to be used in all member states of the European Union but for the purposes of this project focus was on the introduction of a European dimension to English classrooms using the EPBC materials. But because of national curriculum requirements in England and the National Literacy Strategy, it was of paramount importance to consider how these materials could also be used to teach language and literacy. To this end, activities have been designed for use alongside the books which will concentrate not only on the cultural aspects but also on linguistic and literary elements. It is the visual narratives from each of the member states of the European Union that are at the heart of the project. They allow for universal readings of the texts and have the potential, in the hands of creative and dedicated teachers, to play a vital role in injecting a European dimension into the upper primary curriculum.

3

A European dimension in education was first conceived in 1957, when France, Germany, Italy, Belgium, Luxembourg and the Netherlands developed economic links through the *Treaty of Rome*, thus creating the European Economic Community (EEC) – known first as the Common Market and later as the EC. In 1973, Denmark, Ireland and the UK joined the EC, followed by Greece in 1981, Portugal and Spain in 1986 and Austria, Sweden and Finland in 1995 (Lamb, 1997:2). The fifteen countries of the EC that were member states in 1995 were financed by the European Commission to contribute to the European Picture Book Collection (Cotton, 1996).

Directives from the European Commission and recommendations by the Department for Education argue for a European dimension to national curricula and increasingly emphasise the importance of developing materials for use in both teacher training establishments and schools. These materials should reflect not only the national and cultural identity of each country but also a universal world of childhood with which children throughout the European Community can identify and empathise.

Pedagogical innovation and educational change such as this does not just happen. For schools to be able to implement new directives, teachers and teacher educators need to consider how to provide expertise and advice as well as materials at local, regional and national levels. *Picture Books Sans Frontières* discusses some of the possible ways forward and makes links with the very first picture book creator, Comenius – a true European who in 1658 saw the linking of pictures and text as a way of helping children learn independently. In *Picture Books Sans Frontières* European visual narratives are seen as catalysts within the Europeanisation process, and the ways in which picture books can be used in schools parallel Hellawell's perception that: 'The European dimension in education consists of all those curricular and extra curricular elements which heighten the pupils' awareness of themselves as Europeans.' (in: Beernaert, Van Dijk and Sander, 1993: 54).

4   The European dimension does not exist – it has to be created, worked out through debate and collaboration. In the 1993 Treaty of the Commission of the European Union (Maastricht), Article 126/2 states that this collaboration should be developed by encouraging the mobility of students and teachers. Mobility is defined both physically and intellectually (Ogden, 1994: 111). In reality only about 10% of students and teachers have the opportunity to visit other countries, so the focus needs to be on the 90% who may never travel but for whom an understanding of Europe is just as important. This is why intellectual mobility is a vital factor within a European dimension in education.

Intellectual mobility facilitates an understanding of Europe with its similarities and differences, giving individuals the ability to discern and use appropriate suggestions from other Europeans. Picture books can provide a context and a purpose as, through them, European children can learn more about each other. Education has now been brought centre stage and the need to create a social Europe seems to have replaced a purely economic alliance. Education is a vehicle for the policies of the EC and teachers need guidance and relevant materials to use in the classroom. *Picture Books Sans Frontières*, in focusing on both the implementation of a European dimension in the upper primary curriculum and creating materials to support the teaching of language and literature in English classrooms, offers a potential model for fellow member states to incorporate European picture books into the learning programmes and curriculum requirements of their own education systems.

Chapter Two
After Comenius:
European Picture Books

T he picture book as we know it today derives from a range of European influences. The concept of using pictures to illustrate a story is a defining feature of children's literature. This chapter traces its development since the 17th Century and focuses on the pedagogic and literary changes and the political, social, linguistic and cultural effects on the genre. Throughout history, European authors and illustrators have been developing 'machines for creating possible worlds' (Eco, 1981: 264) that transport readers into literary worlds which are shared across nations. What constitutes a good picture book is thus defined.

Although most European countries can claim one or two isolated examples of books published specifically for children following the invention of the printing press, it was not until after Comenius' first picture book that the ideas of the philosopher John Locke were applied. His *Thoughts Concerning Education* (1693) created the possibility of combining pleasure with instruction in literature. A century later, the ideas of Rousseau began to permeate children's literature throughout Europe.

European children's literature really began to flourish in the 19th Century when populations were growing rapidly, educational opportunities were increasing and technological developments becoming economically viable. Previously many European countries, e.g. England, France and Germany, had seen the concept of books for children develop, commonly using traditional folk tales such as told by Perrault and the Brothers Grimm. Creative and imaginative literature flourished in the latter 19th century and there was a move towards universal education. Developments in modern technology created the possibility for more sophisticated illustrations to embellish picture books; it was also at this time that the burgeoning middle classes began to travel. Becoming familiar with the major European languages and receptive to more new ideas, the developing 'reading class' unquestioningly accepted translations of illustrated children's books.

In the twentieth century, children's literature in Europe has been more seriously influenced by politics and war. Not the First World War but the dictatorships which followed in Germany, Italy, Spain and Portugal affected children's literature. From 1928 to 1974 in Portugal, topics in children's picture books were severely limited by dictatorial power (Rocha,1996: 2). The earlier struggles for independence in Finland and Norway also affected picture book content (Westin, 1996: 1). And in England after the Second World War, a more child-centred approach to education, prompted by such figures as Bertrand Russell and A.S. Neill meant that, in children's books, the world was beginning to be seen through the eyes of children.

One of the defining features of children's literature is its incorporation of pictures into the narrative. The concept of using pictures to illustrate a story is well established, although the picture book as we know it has a relatively short history. British illustrator Randolf Caldecott (1846-1886) is widely credited as the first author and artist to develop the level of interplay between picture and text. Credit also goes to printer Edmund Evans (1826-1905) who did much to raise standards in colour printing through his work with Caldecott, Kate Greenaway (1846-1901) and Walter Crane (1845-1915). Picture books rose to new levels at the hands of artists such as Brian Wildsmith and Charles Keeping who, by the 1970s, found their talents served by new colour printing technology. Understatement and irony became something of a stock in trade for many of the best book artists in Britain, and the 'possibilities of transforming seemingly straightforward text into rich comedy was, and still is for most European author/illustrators of the nineties, fully exploited' (Coghlan, 1996: 30).

The picture book at the beginning of the 21st century is very different from that conceived by Jon Amos Comenius in 1658. First and foremost an educational reformer and a campaigner of education for all, Comenius produced a systematic curriculum which included an empirical method of instruction together with physical training. It was whilst working as a master in a Hungarian poor-school that he conceived *Orbis Sensualium Pictus* and, through his interest in teaching languages by direct method, the revolutionary 'picture book' vocabulary of Latin was born. This method, learned from philosophers of the time, was based upon the observation of the actual world – contrary to the purely abstract method of teaching that prevailed. Children whose minds had been crammed with facts that bore no relation to their everyday lives could relate to Comenius' little book, with its attractive woodcuts. 'Even Goethe, who was a child 100 years after its first appearance, mentions *Orbis Pictus* as the first picture book he was to treasure' (Hürlimann, 1967: 132).

Many European educationalists since Comenius have influenced the development of the contemporary picture book but even before *Orbis Pictus* was conceived, writers, illustrators, artists and story-tellers created their

Figure 1: A page from *Orbis Sensualium Pictus*, (Keiffer, 1995: 83)

tales. In 1550, for example, Europe's earliest illustrated fairy stories *Piacevoli notti* were set down on paper in Italy by Giovan Francesco Strapola. During the ancient Greek, Roman and Byzantine eras, and during the Turkish domination of Greece (1453-1821), stories had been transmitted orally and only later written down and illustrated for posterity (Anagnostopoulos 1996: 1). Tales such as these express every nation's feelings for stories; they also embody an international European literature, made possible by the increasing involvement of translators.

Orbis Sensualium Pictus was read throughout Europe and extensively translated from the original Latin. The English version reached England only a year after its first publication. Perrault's tales (1697) followed, with translations from the French permeating Europe. The Brothers Grimm (1812-14) reworked many of these French tales into German, adapting and adding to an already rich source of children's stories; their works also traversed the continent, with stories such as *Little Red Riding Hood* reaching England by 1823. About this time a reverse trade was also operating, with the earlier novels of *Robinson Crusoe* (1719) written by England's Daniel Defoe, and *Gulliver's Travels* (1726) by the Irish writer Jonathan Swift, being translated from English in the mid-nineteenth century.

Giambattista Basile's *Lo cunto de li cunti* first appeared in Neapolitan dialect between 1634 and 1636. These fairy stories, which began in the oral story-telling tradition, were only printed after Basile's death in 1632, in an attempt to preserve the cultural mores of the time. They were primitive, entirely original tales told by the women of the district to their children. These stories were an expression of the Baroque Age and portrayed the truth of the period through dialogue which alluded to contemporary life. Although filled with complicated intrigue, 'right' always triumphed in the end.

While these stories were being told in Italy, in the German speaking part of Switzerland old customs led to the production of a kind of picture book very different from *Orbis Pictus*. In 1645, a New Year's custom in Zürich of giving sweetmeats in return for wine at local drinking houses was changed. Instead of sweetmeats, a copperplate engraving with a short poem underneath – the very first *Neujahrsstücke* – was given. As the years passed, other Swiss communities followed the tradition, and in 1657 Conrad Meyer, a Zürich painter, issued a complete book of engravings and poems. He was the first person in Switzerland to create a picture book for children. Like *Orbis Pictus*, a year later, the book was the first of many such picture books which continued to be developed until the middle of the 19th Century.

The publication of *Emile* by French philosopher, Rousseau, in 1761 had consequences for both children's literature and education, because of his belief that it was the power of images which was crucial in holding children's attention. Rousseau's outlook on the world of pictures allowed children to pass 'from the world of nature to that of culture' (Perrot, 1996a: 4). After this, there followed a number of enjoyable and instructive picture books which brought a completely new world for children into the home. One important addition to this genre was *Elementawerk* by Johann Bernhard Basedow, published in 1770 and influenced by the writings of Rousseau. Each sheet in the three volumes of text contained two to four pictures, presenting things of interest specifically to children: games, drama, historical and biblical stories. Several educationalists in Germany and Switzerland later used Basedow's material, including German teacher Joachim Heinrich Campe. A devotee of *Emile*, Campe tended to embody Rousseau's thinking about natural education.

Sometime between 1782 and 1786, a penniless schoolmaster, I.K.A. Musäus, published a number of volumes in his collection of fairy stories, *Die Volksmärchen der Deutschen*. Following the success of these stories, he published his picture book series, *Folktales, a Story Book for Children Great and Small* which brought the world of the Middle Ages to life. Each story is told with a cheerfulness not found in the tales of Perrault. A decade later, in 1796, Bertuch's *Bilderbuch* appeared. This picture book for children returned to the more naturalistic approach of the earlier part of the century and contained collections of animals, fruits, minerals, and materials from the realms of nature, art and science. With text in German, French, English and Italian, this was a truly European picture book. Readers, however, were expected to read only one page at a sitting, lest they be overburdened with visual stimuli.

At the beginning of the 19th Century Heinrich Pestalozzi in Switzerland began to sway educational thinking away from Rousseau's ideas, with his model of economic and social improvements, especially in his educational writings for the young, *Lienhard und Gertrud* (1781) (Rutschmann 1996: 1). His Swiss colleague, Johannes Fröbel, did the same. Their theories on mother-child relationships and pre-school education were to influence much

Figure 2: *Bilderbuch für Kinder*, Friedrich Johann Justin BERTUCH, Weimar, 1796.
A hand-coloured engraving on 'Air Transport' (in Hürlimann, 1967: 87).

9

early education in the following centuries and inspired many educational picture books which supported their philosophies.

Unsurprisingly one of the first children's books to gain truly international acclaim was Johann David Wyss's *Swiss Family Robinson* (1812). Wyss, a Swiss, much travelled army chaplin and later pastor, spent much of his time writing and illustrating stories to educate his four sons. The exceptional success of his children's story stems largely from focus on children and their personal adventures. Wyss uses comic imagination to portray Swiss practicalities, too. The book has fallen out of favour because of its unquestioning assumption of the superiority of the white 'race'.

Also in 1812, the Brothers Grimm published *Kinder und Hausmärchen*, described as 'butterfly catching' by the French literary historian Paul Hazard (1932), who recognised the importance of the 'specimens' being captured alive. This was very much the way that these two erudite men collected their tales, many of them from a busy farmer's wife in a local German village. They saw themselves as collectors, writing their 1812 version for an adult audience. It was not until 1814 that the children's illustrated edition was published, transmitting a patriotic fervour through their stories and creating part of their nation's heritage, earning worldwide acclaim.

Hans Christian Andersen, now universally renowned as a storyteller, was much influenced by the Brothers Grimm, and the three men met on a number of occasions. Andersen travelled widely and had many literary contacts in France and England, where he gained great popularity. Charles Dickens, seven years his junior, was a friend and colleague, as was Charles Kingsley whose *Water Babies* shows influences from Andersen's fairy tale world. Kingsley also never questions but merely reflects the prejudiced attitudes of the time.

Andersen's stories, based on his own somewhat impoverished childhood memories, have been said to create pictures without pictures, capturing the imagination of the young and inviting them into his 'vividly drawn' secondary worlds through the language of his prose. These 'visual' tales also relate to the animals and nature of his homeland. Andersen loved the wild flying swans of his native Denmark and, in a short story *The Swan's Nest*, likened Denmark to the nest of these beautiful creatures; allusions to these swans are also found in his famous *The Ugly Duckling*, published in 1827. Andersen brought to the European fairy tale an irony and psychological subtlety. The way in which dead things are invested with a soul, learn to speak and become creatures in their own right, has greatly influenced European story-telling and picture book imagery. He is also one of the first writers for children whose stories have tragic endings: the tin soldier in The *Little Match Girl* melts and the eponymous heroine freezes.

When Andersen's stories became popular in Germany, they were not yet readily available throughout Europe, still less in picture book format. It was not until 1871 that they could be obtained in countries such as Spain (Surrallés *et al*, 1996: 1). When the German doctor, Heinrich Hoffman went out to look for a picture book for his three year old son's Christmas present in 1844, he could find nothing suitable. So he came home with a blank exercise book and, just in time for the festivities, completed writing and illustrating *Struwwelpeter*. The central character in this tale is a figure of great importance, whose bizarre bedtime antics made him popular with children throughout Europe. The originality of the drawings and novelty of the mischievous characters show a directness of expression not before seen in children's picture books. Hoffman created many other picture books for his children and grand-children but none achieved the international acclaim of his first – maybe because they did not stem from real situations.

For the same reason that Hoffman wrote *Struwwelpeter*, so the Swiss Jeremias Gotthelf wrote *Der Knabe des Tells*. He felt sorry for children who had to read the moralistic books of the time so he wrote a family story set in the context of contemporary European history. Dealing with the relationship of a father and son, in the Swiss mountainside the story came alive in a new way. The myth of Tell, whose famous shot at the apple had intrigued children worldwide, was now transferred to his son.

In the same year, 1846, Edward Lear's *A Book of Nonsense* was first published in England. The particular appeal of his verse-stories lies in their illustrations, which show Lear to be a great connoisseur and portrayer of nature. What he is most respected for is the fine linguistic quality of his verse and his extraordinarily expressive vocabulary, particularly when read aloud. His greatest achievement, however, is probably the limerick; nonsense literature which imbues animals, people and things with a crazy life of their own, enabling Lear to lead the reader away from reality into a fantasy world. Three years later the first comic picture book for children, *Münchener Bilderbogen*, was written in Germany. Many contemporary 'picture-sheets' developed from this throughout Europe but its greatest influence was in France.

In 1862, eighteen years after Hoffman had written *Struwwelpeter*, Charles Ludwig Dodgson was persuaded by Alice, the youngest daughter of his Dean of Mathematics at Oxford, to write down the stories he had told her. Their success needs no discussion. Dodgson/Lewis Carroll's 'nonsense' tales of *Alice in Wonderland* have been analysed academically throughout Europe and have influenced much contemporary storytelling for young children. Unlike Andersen, whose poetic use of language enabled him to relate his many tales to the children around him, Dodgson wrote his stories for one child. These books, like Hoffman's *Struwwelpeter*, are the work of an original mind. Intensity of thought and feeling permeated his style, producing stories with remarkable penetration.

In the following year, Charles Kingsley's *The Water Babies* was published. Its main character is a destitute little chimney sweep, who takes centre stage and moves young readers to pity through his actions, which transcend the traditional fairy tale. The book has become a European classic. Intended to have political repercussions, as children were often sold or hired out by their parents or simply sent to the workhouse, Kingsley's story appears to have been influenced by the earlier novels of Dickens, such as *Oliver Twist,* published in 1838. Dickens' child characters also confronted readers with the social problems caused by the industrial revolution, the growth of cities and the treatment and status of children.

One year later, in Germany, a picture style was created that was very different in tone. *Max und Moritz* for the first time depicted in pictures a crazy series of antics which many children wanted to emulate. It was quite a surprise to Wilhelm Busch, their creator and a renowned artist, when his two good-for-nothing characters so captivated children. Such an element of malice had not appeared before in children's books, yet it was more successful than any of his other books. The tales of these two characters have become prize possessions in many German households, and have influenced the development of today's contemporary picture books. It is probably no coincidence that the influential work of Frantz Pocci (1807-76), based on the literature of the Punch and Judy shows, was then at its most popular.

One of the most popular and significantly 'travelled' stories of the 19th Century is Carlo Collodi's *L'Avventure di Pinocchio*, first published in about 1883. This animated wooden puppet tale has now been translated into most languages of the world. (The ethics of translations are discussed in Chapter Three). *Pinocchio* is a southern European variant of a fantasy theme, where a wooden puppet comes to life in a world where poverty and riches, ugliness and beauty can all be found. The story is set in the real world where this imaginary character can be seen as a symbol of down-to-earth understanding, providing an exaggerated plot not too far removed from the world of reality. It is the mixture of reality, cheekiness and imagination which gives the book its universal appeal but it is particularly loved by the Italians.

Another very influential book which reflected the values of the time and the prevailing attitudes towards disability is *Heidi*, written by Johanna Spyri and published in Switzerland in about 1880. Only after the universal acclaim this book received did Swiss children's literature begin to cross the borders into Europe and beyond. Although a semi-religious tract, Heidi became an attraction for children all over the world through its sympathetic portrayal of its young heroine, its treatment of homesickness and its superb descriptions of Swiss scenery. What in Johanna Spyri had been new and unique now became a general Swiss style.

Although not as generally well known as *Heidi* or *Pinocchio, Cuore* written by Edmondo de Amicas in 1886, was one of the most important Italian books written for children at that time. Amicas, whose name now fronts a renowned children's library in Genoa, was 'a militant socialist who had the task of encouraging the spread of reading in nineteenth century Italy' (Kreyder, 1996: 2). He intended *Cuore* to raise political awareness among young Italians and it relates the experiences of children in a Turin state school in the newly united Italy. A new boy from Calabria joins a class and the teacher explains how the country had to fight for fifty years and thirty thousand Italians had to die, so that this boy could attend their school. Though so strongly patriotic, the book preaches tolerance towards differences within a nation, and has become a classic of children's literature.

It was not until the 20th Century that children's literature began to appeal directly to children rather than adults. The turn of the century was marked in Sweden by Ellen Kay's famous manifesto, significantly entitled *Barnets århundrade* (*The Year of the Child*) where the important role that illustrated texts play in children's learning was discussed. After its publication, teachers throughout the country launched various projects to promote reading (Westin, 1996: 9). One of the most prolific and influential Swedish picture book creators of this period was Elsa Beskow. Her naturalistic picture books such as *Putte i blåbärsskogen* (*Putte in the Blueberry Wood*), published in 1901, were unrivalled in her own country and became a landmark in the picture book world. Ironically, Beatrix Potter's first picture book was published privately in the same year and, after its success, Frederick Warne Publishers took on her work. Although her tales depicted animals in their natural settings, she often clothed them and anthropomorphised their behaviour but each story generally ends with the animals restored to their natural state.

Die Wiesenzwerge (*The meadow dwarves*), published in Switzerland in 1902, was to fulfil the demands of revolutionary educationalist Walter Crane. This picture book made Ernst Kreidorf, a painter from Berne, famous. There is scarcely a picture book from Switzerland which does not reflect the beauty of its mountainous countryside and Kreidorf's dynamic illustrations were well received. In his early work he depicts a dwarf living in the natural world and complements his poetic text with a picture clarity that greatly influenced picture book production.

13

Not all early 20th Century picture books reflected nature. In 1903, Paula Dehmel's *Rumpumpel* proved significant in mirroring artistic developments in Germany before the first world war. The pictures are an expression of the child's most intimate world and, although apparently more directed towards mothers than children, the oversized illustrated pages retain a feeling for childhood. Carl Larssen's large picture book *Ett Hem (At Home)*, published in Stockholm in 1904, became a household possession for many European families, relating amusing tales of a typical Swedish family, illustrated in a style reminiscent of Busch. Also in 1904, the artistic skill of M. Boutet de Monvel of France generated *Anatole*. His bold line drawings with their pastel colouring brought Anatole the mouse international acclaim, especially in Europe.

In 1932, *The Albums of Père Castor* were published in France. The principle of guiding and educating children by using pictures, which had passed through many stages since Comenius, was now reinstated in these post-war stories. Castor had an inestimable influence on the development of the modern children's picture book; his tales were told in the language of the child, using modern illustrative techniques which held the reader's attention. He began with animal stories but later developed books which related to children from different countries, as he was keen to foster children's learning about other cultures at an early age. His books were aimed at young children who were just beginning to read, because he felt this was a receptive period when the foundations of intellectual development were laid. In his own words:

> *Je crois que la lecture intelligente, celle qui éclaire et enrichit esprit, dépend non seulement de l'acquisition du mécanisme de la lecture, mais de toute une 'éducation préalable'. Cette éducation préalable, cette pré-lecture est précisément la raison d'être de certain de nos albums.* (Hürlimann, 1967: 137/8)

Here Castor is suggesting that the intelligent reader who wishes to improve his mind depends not only on the mechanical acquistion of reading skills but also on preliminary education. This preliminary education, in the form of pre-reading activities, is what his picture books are for.

One of the most popular French children's picture book creators is Jean de Brunhoff, author of *L'histoire de Babar* (1931), *Le Voyage de Babar* (1932) and *Le Roi Babar* (1933). In *King Babar*, Babar rules his welfare state for elephants and is beset by every kind of disaster; his kingdom is not the France of 1933, the year when the first book appeared, nor the France of today, but a never-never land (not unlike that of Peter Pan) where goodness triumphs over disaster. In *Babar en Famille* (1938), the last book he wrote before he died at the age of 38, Brunhoff creates what is probably the most intimate of his books, reflecting as it does his own family life. His son

Laurent continued in his father's footsteps, but there is a clear difference in both the quality of artistic style and the storytelling. The Babar books of 'père et fils' are still popular despite their outdated colonialism and racism and were a milestone in the development of European picture books.

Les Contes du Chat Perché, first published in 1934, contained stories, written by Marcel Aymé, that mixed fable, fairy tale and straight story. As popular as Babar, they are some of the most widely read books in France. Achieving popularity with a completely different theme is Ferdinand, an unusual picture book by Munroe Leaf, published in about 1935. Prize bull Ferdinand refuses to enter the ring to fight, so becoming a symbol for the hatred of war. In 1937 *Das Wunderhaus* (*The house of wonders*) appeared, a picture book with more overtly pedagogic intentions conceived by Seidmann-Freud, in which each activity was backed up by a suitable text so that children could learn through play.

Pippi Langstrump arrived in 1945. Astrid Lindgren's Swedish creation delighted children worldwide with her unorthodox antics, while many adults deplored her behaviour and modern critics object to Lingren's racist attitudes. Teachers found it difficult to accept her non-attendance at school, even though Pippi fulfilled suppressed childhood dreams. But her pranks are neither stupid nor damaging: she is always willing to help people weaker than herself and, above all, she is never boring! In contrast to the 'eternal child' of *Peter Pan,* Pippi is a 'super-child', presenting her readers with a view of childhood as an exciting experience to be relished. Finnish Tove Jansson's *Moomin* books have been translated and adapted for radio and television world wide. Jansson's dwarf-like creatures distinguish themselves from traditional fairy stories about trolls by their origins, which lie neither in reality nor tradition. Immediately popular in Scandinavia when they appeared in the 1940s, these books have travelled well and are widely read in most European countries.

15

Antoine de Saint-Exupéry's *Le Petit Prince* has also traversed Europe. This fascinating picture book appeared in 1945, although its conception dates back to 1940, the year France lost its freedom. The little prince was born in a year of darkness and sorrow, when his creator's country was occupied, so it is no coincidence that he came from a planet which had never been occupied. The little prince is a figure of courage who has given up his life to save his soul. There is a sadness which pervades the book, recognised throughout Europe, especially when the young prince speaks of his own death. Saint Exupéry has clearly been influenced by the tales of Andersen in creating a tragic ending, yet there are elements in his writing which mirror the improbability of Lewis Carroll.

In *Marcelino, Pan y Vino*, written by Sanchez-Silva (Spain, 1952) acceptance of death is taken up in a way that is both modern and rooted in popular tradition. Marcelino, an orphan, keeps small creatures and displays a love of blood and death in the elaborate way that he kills them; an expression perhaps of early preliminaries to bullfighting. He also tells lies and ultimately steals in order to bring bread and wine to a Christ figure which comes to life before the child's eyes, finally taking him to death – the door to true life. This picture book, paralleled only by *Le Petit Prince*, has achieved international fame and become part of the Spanish heritage, bringing transcendental meaning to everyday life. In early writings for children, good conduct was the easiest way of getting to heaven; life counted for little and heaven for everything. An early death meant entry into paradise, and this idea prevailed in puritan England and most European countries until the 19th century. In Catholic countries such as Spain the concept lingered longer; *Marcelino, Pan y Vino* was quite revolutionary in allowing God to be revealed through its protagonist's rather suspect actions.

During the 1940s and 1950s, a number of countries began to receive monies from their governments to improve the status of children's literature. Wales, for example, established Welsh medium primary schools in 1940, which created a demand for Welsh language picture books, the response to which is evident in the pattern of publishing over the last forty years (Williams, 1996: 1). After the Second World War, interest in children's books grew in the Netherlands, where concern about cultural and social 'decay' among children and young people led to the setting up of the '*Bureau Boek en Jeugd*' (*Book and Youth Bureau*) to supply information about children's books (de Vries, 1996: 3). In the 1950s Germany began to catch up with all elements of children's literature, in a belated philanthropic or reforming educational trend. The work of literary scholar Anna Krüger was influential in developing a highly productive period of writing for German children (Ewars, 1996: 7). In Austria, too, children's literature began to flourish, especially artistic picture books (Binder, 1996: 4).

Throughout the remainder of the 1950s and into the 1960s, a number of Southern European countries, including Spain, were stifled with dictatorships which largely controlled both education and children's book production, whereas Northern Europe became prolific. In 1955, for example, a Norwegian, Thorbjørn, revived the genre with his *Robbers of Cardemon*, which even found its way into school libraries. In the same year *Vevi* by German storyteller Erika Lillegg, highlighting rich potentialities in children's lives after the war, became a classic. In 1956, *Die Märchen des Barba Plasch*, stories by a contemporary Swiss storyteller, were recorded by Leza Uffer in German in Zürich. Barba Plasch, whose father had been a celebrated storyteller, continued the tradition by plying his cobbler's trade from house to house and telling fairy stories laced with the specific characteristics of his mountainous locality and the modern world.

In 1956 a series of picture books adapted from films was published in France, creating visual reality from photographs. One of these was Albert Lamorrisse's *Le Balon Rouge*, a delightful visual story of a young boy who is befriended by a red balloon. And Maurice Druon's *Tistou* (1957) provided French children with a character to match *Le Petit Prince, Peter Pan* and *Pippi Longstocking* in a naturalistic picture book which celebrated the advantage of having green fingers. *Mein Urgrossvater und Ich*, published in Germany in 1959 and written by James Krüss, is yet another popular book provoking children to play with words alongside the visual images. Krüss's last book, *Timm Thaler* (1962), has as its theme a child who sells not his shadow but his laughter. Although rather sombre in tone, this story has travelled widely and was recently adapted for British television.

Throughout Europe since the 1960s efforts have been made to render the entire visual world in pictorial terms. The passion for pictures and graphic representation has given rise to many superb achievements in educational resources, and the vast number of quality picture books produced is likely to provide a unifying element for the European dimension. The picture book, now a recognised genre, has become part of a universal childhood heritage available throughout Europe. A picture book such as *Die Geburstagsreise* (*Birthday greetings*) (Walter Grieder, 1961), for example, tells of a birthday journey along the Rhine. Its illustrations strongly emphasise a theme which helps to create unity among different countries and is representative of possibilities for creating greater European understanding through the medium of the picture book. This theme, along with a more detailed analysis of the development of the picture book over the last two decades, is discussed in the next chapter.

17

Chapter Three
Contemporary European Picture Books and Children's Learning

This chapter focuses on the latter 20th Century when European picture books had become more established within educational literature in their own right. Elements or criteria which together make a good picture book are discussed in terms of: visual communication, the creation of secondary worlds, a European community of readers, linguistic diversity and the role of translation. Finally, a case is made for the importance of the travel-ability of picture books and for recognition of their ability to enhance the learning process.

Over the last three decades, in practically all member states in the European Community, picture books have emerged which have a new voice, a way of communicating with young children and inviting them into secondary worlds. Often it is within these worlds that children begin to learn more about themselves and the countries in which they live. Within the picture books' textual and visual imagery there is an opportunity for children to absorb and consider a range of cultural beliefs and expectations on which to lay the foundations of their own personal and cultural identity. The more successful picture books are those which show recognisable aspects of the world children know, as well as those outside their own experience. They combine the known with the unknown through interaction of picture and text, to create new secondary worlds to which children and the adults with whom they share the books can relate.

Visual images dominate children's early learning in all societies, capturing their emotions and imaginations and helping them develop their under-standing of their own culture. Children's growth in literacy is bound up with how they learn to look and what they expect to see (Meek, 1991). Picture books are thus representations of reality, and children's early reading development depends on how they have come to read these pictorial repre-sentations in conjunction with the text. It is the interaction of picture and text, the polysemic nature of picture books and their very heterogeneity and flexibility (Lewis, 1996) that make them such powerful aids to learning. Marie-Louise Fitzpatrick's *The Sleeping Giant*, published in Ireland in 1991, exemplifies this. It concerns the island off the Kerry coast which, legend has it, is really a giant asleep. The twentieth century awakening of the giant shows the old Ireland meeting the new in a series of cartoon-style pictures. Books such as this are vital for children, as they not only capture the familiar but also show that it is changing (Coghlan, 1996:30).

Of paramount importance in the worlds depicted in European picture books is their visual magnetism. Visual literacy and the value of picture books has been widely acknowledged (e.g Moebius, 1986; Nodelman, 1988, Doonan, 1993). The possibilities of real narrative interaction between text and pictures are enormously exciting, but we have to understand how it works (Pullman, 1989). The pictures are part of the whole literary experience: they give children what Doonan calls an 'affective visual experience'. Through their expressive powers, she argues, pictures enable the book to function as an object, something which gives focus to ideas and to which we can attach personal thoughts. By playing with these ideas we create a society of our own (Doonan, 1993). Picture books positively invite personal exploration by each reader in order to reach an interpretation imbued with their life experiences and the resonance of their own previous reading (Wallen, 1990).

Young children are capable of successfully identifying intertextual links of both a written and illustrative nature (Bromley, 1996) and it is this ability that the truly great writers and illustrators exploit. In the best picture books different or complementary messages can be tracked in word and picture, affording many layers of meaning (Gibbs, 1986). These multi-layers invite readers to create a personal world of literary surprises (Perrot, 1996b) and extend their experiences and knowledge of life through encountering other kinds of places, periods, people and situations (Marriott, 1991). Picture books also help to develop children's thinking and often deal with emotions and personal relationships such as jealousy, fear, anger, friendship, family conflict and death.

At best, text and pictures are interwoven: neither text nor picture predominates, rather one complements the other and together they express meanings which could not be conveyed by words or pictures alone. One might say that the pictures nudge the plot along, showing what might not easily be told, but in a manner which demonstrates respect for the reader. In many European countries, as discussed in Chapter Two, the picture book eventually became established as something of an art form. In general, less attention was paid to the text and the story was frequently told through techniques borrowed from the cinema and cartoon art. Currently, however, the importance of the interaction between these two fundamental elements of picture books is becoming recognised as integral to the reading process.

Children are capable of making sophisticated interpretations of picture books, reading between the lines and pictures, understanding layers of meaning, absorbing a wide range of cultural meaning, cross referring to other texts, filling in gaps and generally handling various shades of complexity with apparent ease (Watson and Styles, 1996). Assuming that cultural ways of seeing are shared and that visual representations are common in a society, children are normally attracted by images which reflect both their immediate worlds and the unknown (Graham, 1990). From this visual imagery, they begin to make sense of the world around them and absorb the norms of their own culture. If we are to begin to create a European community of young readers who will learn from each other, can we assume that all children share the same ways of seeing? It surely depends on the texts selected and the ways in which the books are shared. Elaine Moss, in an interview with Janet and Allan Ahlberg, asks: 'Did anyone ever tell you that nowadays picture books must have a universality about them in order to invite the oh-so-necessary sale of international rights; that local colour is therefore a disaster?', so deploring a tendency for publishers to suppress cultural identity in favour of the lucrative international market. Why then has *Peepo*, set in working-class wartime Britain, become such a truly international success? It is, Elaine Moss suggests, because part of the book's charm resides in what Allan Ahlberg calls *a certain particularity*, an invitation into a complete, secondary world (Moss, 1990).

21

It is this certain peculiarity, this invitation to enter into complete worlds exemplified in well chosen and powerful picture books, which supports the rationale for using picture books with upper juniors, discussed in Chapter Four. The stories we tell our children and the narratives we give them to make sense of their cultural experience, suggests Watkins (1992: 194), constitute a 'kind of mapping, maps of meaning that enable our children to make sense of the world. Such stories contribute to children's sense of identity, an identity that is simultaneously personal and social'. Pictures can express moods and meanings, whole periods or cultures, and can evoke not just what they might mean for their original viewers but also what those individuals or periods of culture have come to mean. The starting point for young European readers is, however, likely to depend greatly on the intertextual knowledge – visual, textual, cultural and linguistic – brought to the picture book, which might mean different things for young readers from different countries within the European Community. For example, the 'Englishness of English books', with which Meek (in Cotton 1996: xiv) is so concerned, might well be lost if young readers from other European countries are not alerted to it.

Chambers (1995) suggests it is important for children to have access to European cultures and literature whilst they are still children, and Dunn (1995) argues that children should have access to other European languages at a very early age, too. Traditionally, picture book translation has only been available in some parts of Europe, thus affording limited access to their stories. The problem for the UK, however, has been that the 'traffic' of children's picture books has not been 'two-way'. Whilst other European countries have been publishing up to 35% of picture books from fellow member states, the UK translates only about 1% (Brennan 1996). In addition, the few translations available are often not seen as emanating from other parts of Europe; publishers like Klaus Flugge of Andersen Press (1994), for example, bemoan the insular attitude of the British who, he says, will not buy 'foreign' books unless the protagonist's name has been anglicised. Many English children are not in fact aware that 'their' traditional stories are not English in origin, for example: *Pinocchio* (Italy); *Red Riding Hood* (France); *Heidi* (Switzerland); *Pippi Longstocking* (Sweden), or that the stories of Hans Christian Andersen are Danish and that the Brothers Grimm were German.

'Learning a second language is part of a multi-faceted intercultural learning process which takes place by learning with and from those of other cultures and which relates to every aspect of culture', suggest Satzke and Wolf (1993). This passage introduces the chapter in the Austrian National Curriculum on the teaching of German to 'non-German mother tongue speakers'. The introduction goes on to focus on the importance of the school in fostering respect amongst children for other languages and cultures and the need to prepare children for life (Gregory, 1996: 174). Respect for language and culture is very much the concern of children's picture books, for they are about as well as for children and reveal what a nation believes childhood to be, plus what is right and proper for the young to know! Through the visual storyline of books, children are 'cued in' to the culturally based 'reading secrets', as Meek (1988) calls them, and quickly use new-found skills to decipher the text.

Universal childhood themes are also important when choosing books to foster language learning and cultural awareness. Chambers (1996:11) believes that children can not only cope with brutal realities but that they should consider them precisely because they are *there* – cruelly present in life. Children, he feels, need 'the kind of assistance to understanding that only the redescriptive, the redemptive capacity of narrative can provide', which means exercise of the right to know as well as protection from abuse and exploitation. Children's books are different from books for adults, but they are equally valuable and just as influential in shaping the culture. Through books, children can become aware that they are a nation family. For example in Finland, once it gained independence from Sweden, it was the Finnish language used in children's books which began to strengthen the country's identity. Similarly, Luxembourg has been using a newly found Luxembourgish children's writer to bring back the nation's language and identity to its people (Cotton, 1996). The desire to maintain a dialogue with tradition and pass on a cultural heritage is an important feature of modern children's literature (Westin, 1991:22) and this has been particularly noticeable since the 1980s when many picture books began mixing older texts with new.

Literature in translation can enrich our lives by providing sensitive glimpses into the lives and actions of young people located in other parts of the world. Translated books become windows, allowing readers to gain insights into the reality of their own lives through the actions of characters from other cultures who are very like themselves. 'They frame experiences' suggests Jobe (1996: 411) 'in other cultures vastly different from their own' – although it could be argued that childhood experiences do not vary significantly from one European culture to another. Access to European literature and picture books is likely to enable young Europeans to realise the similarities between their childhood cultures as well as the culturally based differences.

Translations form a major part of our Western literary heritage and European children's literature has been highly influenced by a significant variety of cultures, as discussed in Chapter Two. The Greek and Norse myths and legends have been influential and so have *The Arabian Nights* (from the Arabic: 1712); *The Swiss Family Robinson* (from the German: 1814); Grimm's Stories (from the German: 1823); Andersen's Fairy Tales (from the Danish: 1846); and *Heidi* (from the German: 1884). More recently, the antics of Lindgren's *Pippi Longstocking*; the itchy nose of Collodi's *Pinocchio*; the blunderings of Preussler's *Robber Hotzenplotz* and the foibles of Prøsen's *Mrs Pepperpot* have made their contribution. The tradition of translating literature for young people is a long-standing one in Europe. Europeans who are surrounded by many languages, for example people living in Belgium, Holland and Luxembourg, accept translations as a daily part of their life; between 30% and 70 % of the children's books published in Europe are translated. But this is not the case in English speaking countries. Europe generally considers it important to have books from many countries available for children to read; the same welcoming tradition of translations has not been evident in the UK despite its EU membership.

One of the reasons why publishers are reluctant to include books in translation on their lists is the complex nature of the translation process and the difficulty in finding people qualified to do justice to the original. In the current process, translating literature for children presents a complex challenge wherein the translator tries to capture the original sense and meaning of the story in another language. Anthea Bell, one of the UK's most prestigious

23

translators, for instance of *Asterix*, and who has won the Marsh Award for books in translation, suggests that she always tries to think: 'what would the author have said if s/he had been writing in English in the first place?' (Jobe, 1996: 413). She also explained to me recently that she makes a point of only translating into English, as she feels it important to write in her mother tongue, thus choosing the very best language possible for the audience.

Bell believes that picture books present a real challenge for the translator as 'every word counts' and the correct choice is vital in conveying what the author really wants to say. Rita Oittinan, a Finnish translator, agrees that picture books provide an additional challenge but believes that when the translator sees the original text with certain illustrations, the pictures influence the solutions. This affects not only the choice of words but also the style of writing throughout the book (Oittinan, 1991:15). Thus picture books, although short compared with novels, require an especially accomplished translator to deliver the essence of the writer's and illustrator's intent. Words are at a premium and each one must be precise enough to convey the nuances of the meaning. This is not unlike the problem facing writers of early reading scheme books or indeed authors of the picture books themselves, who have obviously selected the language specifically so that each word in its contextual position conveys a precise meaning.

24 One side effect of the dramatic increase in co-production of picture books from other countries is the fear that writers and illustrators will lower their cultural standards and create works for children so general in nature that they require little or no editorial change from one culture to another. Martin Waddell, for example is Irish, yet writes 'universally' (Dunbar, 1996), possibly at the expense of cultural references. In some cases, writers omit specific places and local character names, are careful about which everyday objects are used, and make only limited references to cultural customs, as in the translation into English of *Johnny My Friend* by Peter Pohl, from the Swedish (Chambers, 1994). Similarly, there is concern that artists will produce illustrations so bland that they do not offend any reader – unfortunately, they are also unlikely to be enriching or stimulating!

Translations into English were very sparse until the 19th Century. The major sources having been Comenius (1658); Perrault (1697/1729); The Arabian Nights (1712); Grimm (1823); Andersen (1846); Hoffmann (1848); Verne (1870/2); Spyri (1894) and Collodi (1891). The years following the Second World War marked a period of intense upheaval, international frustration, inward-focused reconstruction policies, and a general lack of literary communication. The construction of the Berlin wall, a post-war iron curtain, halted the sharing of information about life between the West and many Eastern European countries as well as inhibiting consideration of their views on the struggles during the war years. The continuing effects of the war brought a need for titles that related to the concerns of the people. The 1970s was the beginning of a golden era and saw the rise of professionally translated picture books as an art form. Unfortunately, things changed in the mid-1980s. Although the exchange of titles in translation continued in most areas of Europe, in English speaking countries the interchange became almost entirely with other English speaking countries.

The political changes of the 1990s created uncertainty about the world among adults, and also a sense of uneasiness in young people. It is difficult to understand, suggests Jobe (1996: 414), 'the strong sense of nationalism which exists at the same time when market economies are insisting on larger and larger political units'. How do young people, he asks, 'learn to experience what it is like to live in other cultural areas of the world and how will children learn what it is like to live in a more global community?' There has never been a more important time for children to be able to read books from other areas of the world yet, as Kerrigan (1993: 15) points out, of the 67,704 books published in Britain in 1991, only 1,689 were translations – a mere 2.4%. We remain, says Kerrigan, 'a nation of cultural Euro-sceptics with little interest in looking outward for our reading matter'. Ideally, according to Jobe (1996: 410) 'children need to read the best literature other countries have to offer'.

25

In her article *Does Pinocchio have an Italian Passport?* O'Sullivan (1992) suggests that translation is one of the ways in which texts can be adapted to reach a different culture but she questions the ethics of it and wonders how children will learn from each other if this happens continually. She points out that, for example, in one translation of *Pinocchio* from the Italian to German, even the food changes, plus the climate and the air of magic (1992: 84), and considers a number of other 'Classics' such as *Robinson Crusoe*, *Don Quixote*, *Peter Pan* and *Heidi*, which have all met similar fates. O' Sullivan (1992: 81) suggests that translation is the 'central moment, the pivot between cultures when a work passes from one into the other' and the story is then accepted into the receiving country's canon of literature. Problems do tend to arise, however, over the literary status of these books – are they to be seen as creative works in their own right or simply secondary products which may penetrate the world of childhood?

An awareness of childhood as being intrinsically different from adulthood and thus requiring special treatment, has been a concern of translators for a number of years. Children are affected by the images of childhood they encounter, whether in real life or in various forms of story, suggests Hollindale (1997:14), so they need to meet children outside their actual lives and cultures in order to understand their own position within a wider European context. The potential 'travelability' of stories across Europe has therefore to be carefully considered when choosing books to be shared across cultures, especially if the expression of a culture is so closely bound to its linguistic means of expression that it is impossible to achieve a correspondence in another.

One special characteristic of children's literature, discussed in Chapter Two, is that it is not only governed by literary norms but also belongs to the changing educational world. This has to be taken into account during the translation process, as often changes are made which take the reader away from the original cultural text. Nières (1992) believes that whilst all texts are unquestionably culturally specific in terms of their own origin, some reveal themselves to be more so than others – especially when the culture is made explicit in the book. It is rare that such books get an international readership, except perhaps in the case of a children's novel such as *Heidi* which unmistakably reflects the Swiss countryside and the culture of the time – including punitive attitudes to disability (Saunders, 2000). So a European dimension in education through picture books will be generated by universal themes which permeate the texts. It is these which are likely to provide the stimulus for creative teachers to extend children's education, together with specific classroom activities which will direct children's attention towards their European neighbours.

26

The history of children's literature is also a history of the formulation of childhood images in both classic children's literature and contemporary picture books. The loss of national identity through translation noted by O'Sullivan is precisely the reason for teachers, particularly in England, to discuss the origins of each book they read to their class and indicate the cultures they represent. Educationalists in all countries, especially classroom teachers, have been so crucial to the development of children's literature throughout history that we have now reached a point where teachers and teacher trainers must take responsibility for allowing a European awareness of other cultures to permeate the school systems. Only then can there be less watering down of cultural identity, making it easier to distinguish traits in picture books which relate to the countries of origin. Interchanges of ideas from different cultures may precipitate interesting developments and improvements in overall standards of technique and production, but it would be a great loss if the characteristics which make for interesting cultural differences in picture books are lost in a general blurring into an amorphous, albeit high quality, pan European style (Coghlan, 1996: 31).

Chapter Four
The Potential of Picture Books for Upper Juniors

Ever since Comenius, illustrated texts have been perceived as the domain of young children who may share them with a parent as a first step to reading alone. More recently, however, the potential of picture books is being recognised for older readers. In 1981, Elaine Moss, was making a case for using picture books with 9-13 year olds, suggesting that:

> young people must come to terms with their world which is largely conditioned by the mass media. But opportunities to explore issues raised in those startlingly brief flashes of pictures accompanied by clipped commentary are essential if the adolescent viewer is to become a discerning adult (p.4).

This chapter argues that appropriately chosen picture books have the potential for helping upper junior readers to become more discerning Europeans. It considers definitions of the picture book, its origins and how it works, and focuses on the concepts of childhood and the universal themes that permeate the form. Picture book culture is discussed in terms of the reader's entry into possible secondary worlds of fantasy and reality and, finally, suggestions are made about how European picture books can be used in upper primary classrooms.

There is general agreement that picture books exemplify and adorn the domain of children's literature (Meek, 1996:7). Definitions abound, however, as to what actually constitutes a picture book: are they toys which can be manipulated in a variety of ways or can they develop concepts, inform the reader or tell stories? Whatever the definition, it is clear that pictures have a central educational role, whether alone or supported by different levels of text. Shulevitz (1985:15) argues that a true picture book tells a story mainly or entirely with pictures, and any words have an auxiliary role. Cooney (in Keiffer, 1995: 6) on the other hand, likens the picture book to a string of pearls, where the pearls represent illustrations and the string printed text, creating an interdependency between the two. Keiffer (1995: 6) takes these ideas further and sees the picture book as 'a unique art object, a combination of image and idea, that allows the reader to come away with more than the sum of the parts'.

The picture book is a combination of visual images and verbal text which combine to extend and deepen an apparently simple story by skilfully blending pictures with written language. The reciprocity between visuals and text enables children to enter more fully into the experience of stories which have the potential to bridge the gap between the recognisably oral-tradition and autonomous written expositions. Baker and Freebody (1989: 185-6) suggest that picture books appear to be 'transitional between oral conventions and written conventions of communication' where reported talk represents 'a reshaping of natural oral interaction'. The picture book tradition, they believe, in spite of its encyclopaedic beginnings by Comenius, shows 'preference towards story form, which has antecedents in pre-literate oral cultures, as a type of discourse recruited for literary instruction'.

Picture book stories are to be enjoyed and discussed at a number of levels. They are seldom as straightforward as they appear. Children require a general understanding of what pictures are, before they can read marks on the page as being a character within the story (Nodelman, 1996: 144). They need to know about pictorial conventions so they can translate the qualities of the image into the objects that they represent. Complex and sophisticated assumptions about what pictures do and how viewers should respond to them, he maintains, underlie any picture book reading. Children must know the conventions of picture captioning to realise that the words are pointing them towards a perusal of the contents of the image. Their knowledge of the literary conventions of picture books leads readers to assume that, for example, the speaker is not the character in the story but someone else, a narrator.

28

Such complexities have led many theorists (Moss, 1981; Benton and Fox, 1985; Graham, 1990; Baddeley and Eddershaw, 1994) to suggest that picture books are not only for the very young. Good picture books deal with important human issues and can convey complex ideas despite their economy of words, making them eminently suitable texts for teaching older primary children literary conventions which appear in adult fiction. Picture books, believe Baddeley and Eddershaw (1994: 19) are an effective way of

> moving children towards an appreciation of sub-text and irony... they make visual what more sophisticated texts use language to imply... and give children access to a device which deepens their appreciation of story at a level they can understand.

Often it is possible to make cinematic comparisons. Children generally scan a picture, like the screen, with 'equal attention to all parts' (Nodelman, 1996: 117). So the ability to pick out and focus on a character at the centre is a learned activity, and reinforces important cultural assumptions about objects and people which have different values and require different degrees of attention. Because there are pictures as well as words, their subject positions have much in common with what films offer their viewers (Metz, 1982). The pictures in both media offer 'readers' a position of power and exist only so that we can look at them: they invite us to observe. Much as the film editor chooses the shots and viewpoint to be seen, the picture book illustrator presents salient snapshots of the story with carefully chosen close-ups, midshots and long shots to convey empathy with the characters or tension in the plot. Philippe Dupasquier's *Going West* exemplifies this; he sets the scene in long shot: wagon train participants preparing to set off 'West'. The central family is then introduced – first in close-up and then, as the story unfolds, cleverly chosen visual formats convey movement across double page spreads, as well as intimacy and distance.

Like the actors in a play or film, the characters in most picture books are presented in series of visual images; it is up to the reader to make the personal intertextual links. The power such pictures offer, however, is illusory. We are encouraged to absorb the codes and conventions, the signs that make them meaningful, yet in our own observation, we are enmeshed in a net of cultural constraints. The way children make sense of pictures is, according to Arnheim (1974), through the interplay of tensions between objects which could be seen as 'culturally engendered codes'. Arnheim points out (1969: 49) that the film artist, like the picture book illustrator, 'quite definitely guides the spectator's attention, gives him directions, indicates the interpretation he is to put upon objects'. In films, concurs Perkins, (1972: 71) 'we have to accept the point of view given to us ... We can watch. We can listen. All the rest is in the mind'. Similarly, picture books depend on the thought processes involved during the interplay of visual and auditory images. They convey enjoyment through surprisingly complex means, and communicate only within a network of conventions and assumptions about visual and verbal representations and the real objects they represent. Picture books in general, plus their various components, are what semioticians call 'signs': in Umberto Eco's words (1985:76) 'something (which) stands ... for something else in some respect or capacity'.

Many picture books enable children to take up ways of meaning relevant to literary readings of text, through the patterning of semiotic resources in both language and visual image. The devices that storytellers use are inventive and subtle. They require concentration, interpretation, a knowledge of symbols, an eye for detail and an understanding of certain conventions. Making ourselves and our children more conscious of picture book semiotics will help them to see their world, themselves and the worlds of others with greater perception. Nodelman (1996: 123) suggests that this allows us to give young readers 'the power to negotiate their own subjectivities'. Close attention to picture books automatically turns readers into semioticians; it encourages appreciation of the cleverness of both the visual and verbal artists, develops awareness of signs and symbols and alerts readers to how picture book fictions can at times misrepresent the world.

The hallmark of a good picture book is that it invites response at the symbolic level and is open to interpretation (Baddeley and Eddershaw, 1994: 65). The semiotic patterning of visual texts, frequently using anthropomorphism, helps children to understand at once that this is not simply a story but that it is saying something about life. Children's knowledge of semiotic design generally, but specifically of the visual, is an important base for further insight into how literary texts work. Kress and van Leeuwen (1990), for example, in their analysis of the semiotic resources of visual images, des- cribe the direct gaze from a character to the viewer as one way in which demands, as compared to offers, are made. What follows may, therefore, influence the storyline. In Maurice Sendak's *Where the Wild Things are*, for instance, the significance for narrative development is that Max begins to act in the transformed world of his own room.

Variation in the angle at which characters are depicted can also be a signi- ficant semiotic tactic. The angle of view expresses a relationship of power between reader or viewer and represented image. These visual devices parallel many of the great works of the cinema. Films such as Citizen Kane, directed by Orson Welles in 1941, would not have realised the dominant character of Kane, or his empire, without the angle of view frequently emanating from below, to suggest and create his overpowering world.

The intended audiences for picture books are, by definition, relatively in- experienced and need to learn how to think about their world and how to see and understand themselves and others. Consequently, suggests Nodelman, (1996:116) 'picture books are a significant means by which we integrate young children into the ideology of our culture'. Hollindale (1988: 10) believes that ideology is an 'inevitable, untameable and largely uncontrollable factor in the transaction between books and children', so the ideological content of early reading books can be treated as preparation for adult citizen- ship, where social and cultural values can be explored. But picture books can and often do encourage children to take for granted views of reality that many adults find too fantastic or indeed objectionable or difficult to comprehend.

A consideration of ideology in children's fiction would not be complete with- out noting how children's fiction is becoming a commodity in a global market, controlled by a relatively small number of international publishers. Doonan (1996: 233) suggests that this is the result of the growing demands

30

of international co-operation in the book market, requiring the pictures to be printed in one single large print run and sold to different countries where texts in the relevant languages are attached. She notes the advantages of this process: firstly, it is cheaper for the publishers and, secondly, the 'originality of vision' of most creative artists, writers and designers is made available to all. But there are concerns that writers and illustrators will dilute their cultural references and create works for children so general in nature that they require little, if any, editorial change from one language edition to another (Jobe, 1996: 569).

Texts operate a plurality of codes that leave them open to a plurality of readings (Barthes, 1974) and this it what makes them such a powerful read. Writers and illustrators throughout Europe are becoming increasingly aware of this and realise that children gain satisfaction from identification and participation with the text, as an expansion of their own experience. The metafictional elements found in contemporary fiction have their picture book counterparts, as writers and artists question notions of how stories are told and meanings, conventions and techniques subverted. Often boundaries are broken between fictional characters and the picture books in which they appear, as well as between the writer/illustrator and reader. *Zoem, de zebra*, a delightful picture book by Sylviane Gangloff from Flemish speaking Belgium exemplifies this well. Both the writer and the illustrator conduct an ongoing commentary with the reader. Zoem, eyes front, immediately addresses the reader 'Hello! My name is Zoem!'. As he begins to describe himself, his stripes start to disappear and he calls in the artist to re-paint them. Unfortunately, this illustrator is not well versed in the ways of zebra stripes, and Zoem becomes quite distraught by her ineptitude. Finally the artist manages to paint the stripes correctly – so allowing the reader to reflect on the metafictive game that has been played through the 'bookishness' of the story and the pivotal role of the illustrator.

Metafictive picture books 'prise open the gap' between words and pictures, suggests Lewis (1990: 141), pushing them apart and forcing the readers and viewers to work hard to forge the relationship between them. Children therefore need to be sensitive to the ways in which meaning is represented in picture books. By involving readers in the production of textual meanings, metafictions can teach literary and cultural codes and conventions and hence empower children to read more competently. In metafiction the gap between fiction and reality is made explicit and metafictive dialogue can show readers how representations of reality are constructed and ascribed with meaning. The visual and verbal components of picture books imply a dialogue between text and picture which McCallum (1996: 400) describes as:

a 'bricolage' of visual quotations, which interplay with the text, producing realistic pictorial conventions to represent fantastical situations, blurring textual distinctions between fantasy and reality.

These visual quotations also allow readers to make intertextual links between current texts and those that have been read or experienced earlier. Texts of quotation are probably the simplest level at which child readers can recognise intertextuality, suggests Wilkie (1996:133). These function and are recognised by their allusive qualities because they make explicit assumptions about stories or fairytales which children will know. Intertextuality is a condition of much writing in English. In *The Englishness of English Children's Books* (Cotton, 1996: 152), Meek points out that successful English writers for children, such as the Ahlbergs, are 'counting on the readers' acquaintance with other commonly known stories in English – it is a game for insiders'. Bromley (1996) exemplifies Meek's idea when she explores intertextuality with her class, to see whether they can make explicit their knowledge about intertextual links. For this to be determined, she stresses, careful consideration has to be given not only to the teacher's role but also to the books selected.

Intertextual links discovered by children are not simply of a literary nature. Reading applies to a greater number of representational forms than ever before: pictures, maps, screens, design graphics and photographs are all regarded as vehicles for text. Learning about textuality with young students should therefore be encouraged in order to rebuild and reshape stories and expositions, whether recounting experiences orally, writing from a personal perspective or focusing on other, imagined perspectives. These visual and textual 'clues' can then be heuristically used as a device for shaping discussions which create relations between children and culture in texts. Through explicit knowledge of intertexts, children will have noticeably different experiences of reading and are likely to experience what Barthes (1957: 36) describes as the 'circular memory of reading'. They will begin to relate not only to images which function as the equivalent of simile and metaphor but also intertextuality, returning again and again to characters and actions already discovered in other childhood literary worlds.

Children's fiction rests on the idea that there are children out there to be addressed – but this has not always been the case. Before Comenius' picture book, illustrated texts were created with an adult audience in mind and children were considered as a group apart. Further back into the 10th and 11th centuries, images of childhood were not dwelt upon at all (Ariés, 1973). In medieval society, the idea of childhood did not exist and adult theories about childhood have varied remarkably over the centuries. Definitions of 'childhood' have differed throughout history and from culture to culture, and

32

Ariés suggests that the 'family' and 'childhood' are ideas that function within cultural and social frameworks as carriers of changeable social, moral and ethical values.

There is some commonality of experience of childhood across contemporary European cultures, and European picture books illustrate similar theories and constructions of this theme. They invite tacit acceptance by child readers of particular cultural images of childhood. But young children whose identities as children differ considerably from these embedded images may have difficulties in relating seriously to the books. This is why animals are often used as a metaphor for childhood, with allegorical descriptions treating animals as participants in human-like worlds, thus creating part of contemporary constructions of childhood. Picture books portray a childhood which child readers may or may not recognise but the aim of the texts is generally to achieve some parallel between children's everyday lives and the material they encounter in books.

Drawing attention to characteristics, activities and events by adults can address issues of whether portrayals of social life fit other available descriptions of childhood culture. For child readers, such an interpretation would involve not only an immersion in child-culture but possibly an appreciation of how adults view children. Picture book texts are, in complex and subtle ways, part of each culture's organisation of age relations as well as a reflection of childhood itself. It is the freshness that comes from the picture book creators' understanding of who the child is that enables young readers to relate universally to the genre. The ways visual images are constructed, point out Glazer and Williams (1979), become part of every child's encounters with adult views of how 'children' speak, act and perceive the world. A mixture of reality and fantasy in stories which appear to concern recognisably ordinary people is thus a particularly powerful device for informing children about adult definitions of what it is to be a child.

By their very nature, picture books work to make their audiences aware of the limitations and distortions of their representations of the world and readers need to sort out what kind of possible world the story is to be taken to represent. Texts can present many possible worlds inhabited by diverse characters, whether children or humanised animal-characters. Invitations to compare oneself with the text-characters is a transitional phase, which assists child-adult relations during the exploration of the fictional world. Heap (1985: 265, 266) sees this as taking the text 'off the page and into the culture to turn 'boring maps' into meaningful texts'; where comprehension is building bridges between the new and known. Consequently, children need to be in tune culturally and intellectually with the text and willing to search for a 'cultural logic'.

33

Benton and Fox (1985: 10-15) consider that the process of responding when we read stories involves us in creating a secondary world. The reading experience is characterised in two ways, they suggest. First, a four phase process of feeling like reading; getting into the story; being lost in the book; having an increasing sense of an ending; and second, as an activity consisting of four more elements – picturing, anticipating/retrospecting, interacting, and evaluating. For immersion in this secondary world, however, children need stimulating texts which will make the journey rewarding. An intermingling of picture and myth, narrative and image, plus the inclusion of both fantasy and everyday stories will engage children who are familiar with and receptive to reading both primary and secondary worlds.

Some texts unambiguously enter into a fantasy world – Sendak's *Where the Wild Things are* or Burningham's *Come away from the water, Shirley* – whereas others contain brief, unsignalled and unpredictable sorties into fantasy, often without any implications for the plot. The credible fantasy of Anthony Browne's work illustrates this: his creative visual portrayals of family life, as in *The Tunnel*, have a fantasy element just beneath their surface. His devotees have now come to expect this, and their readings of his worlds become more sophisticated as the intertextuality of his work is discussed, presenting interpretive puzzles for readers. The blending of realistic and fantastic elements in everyday settings in picture books generally challenges readers. Often fantasy and reality elements interweave around the activities of animal characters, who can talk and are part of this fictional everyday life.

34

Alongside these elements, the narrator also mixes realistic and fantastic language into the reported direct utterances of animal characters. Children know that pets do not talk, except in stories or other fantasies, but they join in with the adult construction of child-like playfulness which arises from the obviously unreal nature of reported events. If readers actually 'believed' in this 'reality', the stories would lose their playful value. Children need to know that talking animals, for example, are an element of child culture generally created by adults, and so they have to collude in this fantasy secondary world.

Folk and fairy stories containing speaking animals do seem to have been considered a significant part of child culture. They deal with powerful human emotions that we all have to come to terms with in our lives such as jealousy, insecurity, sibling rivalry, usurpation, feelings of inadequacy and the transforming power of love. These stories help children to come to terms with their own feelings and those of others, much as great literature can illumine the lives of adults. In the words of Bettelheim (1976: 5):

> For a story truly to hold the child's attention, it must entertain him and arouse his curiosity. But to enrich his life, it must stimulate his imagination; help him to develop his intellect and to clarify his emotions; be attuned to his anxieties and aspirations; give full recognition to his difficulties, while at the same time suggesting solutions to the problems which perturb him.

The magical property of books is universal (Olmert, 1992: 23) and the fact that different cultures have stories in which the same elements occur indicates that certain themes have basic human appeal and are universal. Repetitions link children with events and as their language develops, young people learn to discover how their culture endows experience with meaning. Stories read to them become part of their own memories and children borrow characters so as to insert themselves into the continuous 'storying' of everyday events (Meek, 1996:2,3). They also expect some tales to cast light on what they are unsure about: the dark, the unexpected, the repetitious and the way adults behave. Narrative is a 'primary act of mind transferred to art from life' says Hardy (1977:12) and it is reflected in picture books which deal with life-subjects in a wide range of styles and presentations. Topics are generally of current social and moral concern: such as sex, poverty, illness, crime, family styles and disruptions... boundaries that deal with actualities are usually not fixed but blurred. Thus the universal childhood themes which permeate European picture books can often engage young readers at a deeper level than their language will express but which their feelings recognise, allowing development towards an understanding of their own as well as other cultures.

European picture books frequently depict the everyday world of the child by featuring familiar character-types in the stories. Providing readers with definitions of what their identities, interests, attitudes and experiences are conventionally deemed to be can resonate with children's social life and psychological worlds. Specific stereotypes offer recognition and reliability because they invite comparisons and are interesting in themselves. The authors and illustrators determine which categories of character will be described and how membership of those categories will be elaborated within the text, and this establishes the quality of experience to be 'lived'. The nature of the social world depicted in children's picture books can be seen from an examination of the types of characters which most frequently appear in them. Human society is primarily depicted in the home or at school, where the interaction between characters encourages children to reflect on their own experiences and make moral judgements about each character's behaviour.

Picture books are not neutral or content free; they portray characters in social relationships in distinct ways, locating the reader in a particular relationship with book-knowledge and, more broadly, with school learning (Baker and Freebody, 1989: xvii). Once children enter the secondary world of picture books, they become absorbed in interactions between the characters and can reflect on their own experiences, empathising with the actions and feelings of others. The relationships which permeate these imaginary worlds are mostly concerned with generation and kinship, and feature parents, grand-parents, siblings and friends. Professional adult models such as teachers appear much less often; the salient relationships appear to be within the culture or varieties of family life, covering three generations. Picture books often seek to convey a child's gaze on the world and delineate an apparent perspective on the scenes in stories from a specific position within the family.

European children today live in a highly complex visual world and are bombarded with intense visual stimuli, received from around the world. Researchers have realised the potential for picture books to develop visual learning strategies which can evoke a variety of intellectual and emotional responses. But the full potential of European picture books has yet to realised in terms of learning about other cultures through the visual narratives of picture book texts. It is often possible to indicate through pictures things that are difficult to say in words. So the power of the illustrations enables children to appreciate a familiar story in a new way and find deeper layers of meaning. Their need for familiarity with conventions is often exploited to produce complex narrative that is inherent in images: painterly styles include expressionism, symbolism, surrealism, romanticism, pop art and collage.

36

Picture books show children that illustrations and words complement and enhance each other. Mitchell (1986:44), suggests that the relationship between pictures and accompanying texts is 'a complex one of mutual translation, interpretation, illustration and enlightenment'. Illustrators may depict two events simultaneously, so children need to be able to see the relationship between the two narratives. Philippe Dupasquier is a master of this technique; his picture book *Dear Daddy* relates the tale of a child's father going off to sea, while the visuals follow the lives of both characters during the voyage in parallel worlds. Only in the concluding frame, the homecoming, do father and son inhabit the same world. Children need to 'read' the pictures and text together carefully to perceive the interplay between the simultaneous life experiences. The pictures provide information about the actions described in the words. Words in picture books frequently tell us that things are not simply as they appear in the pictures; picture books are inherently ironic and a key pleasure they offer is a perception of the differences in the information offered by visual and auditory 'text' . Maurice Sendak (1988: 185) describes the interaction between picture and text thus:

> You must leave a space in the text so that the pictures can do the work. Then you must come back with the word, and now the word does its best and the picture beats time.

Picture books evoke a highly personal, aesthetic response in readers (Olmert, 1992: 23). Fully understanding the story in quality picture books depends mainly upon the reader's ability to interpret the pictures. Empathy and moral issues can be explored in picture books and the same story may be read in different ways, often creating a new learning experience. It is also possible to wrestle with meaning rather than simply taking things at face value (Benton, 1996: 75), and this makes many illustrated texts suitable for older readers. Indeed Lewis (1990: 131-146), observes that picture books 'anticipate certain *avant-garde* adult novels by questioning the way reality is normally presented in fiction'. Meek (1996: 19) invites us to 'read them with your most adult awareness of life and literature and text, and you will see that the invitations they offer to young readers are far from infantile'.

To increase our understanding of the ways in which literature works for children, we need to probe how they grasp the sorts of textual devices that writers use; their comprehension of rituals within stories builds upon their prior reading and this equips them for more sophisticated texts. In most of the best picture books there is often a metaphor beneath the hilarious surface. Michael Foreman's *War and Peas*, for example, is a thinly disguised pictorial parable about surplus food enjoyed by a rich nation while its poorer neighbours starve, and concludes with the question: 'What is the recipe for peace?'

37

The 'golden rule for teachers' suggested Comenius is that 'everything should, as far as possible, be placed before the senses'. He believed that proper presentation and explanation of pictures would help to make the intimate connection between images, written word and reality. Some three hundred years later, children are still encouraged to look, feel and listen as they make contact with the world around them. The interplay between text and picture and the economic use of words in picture books can, over a period of time, enable teachers to develop children's awareness of the complexity of these narratives, especially their subtext. Teachers who explore the nature of literacy in the classroom, using texts which encourage children to investigate literary meaning-making as textual practice, is crucial to pupils' development. Children appear able to learn for pleasure and for exploration of meaning. Barthes (1974) suggests that children can learn to read while acting as though nothing but the patterning of language was the source of their pleasure. It is the integration of these two forms of pleasure which makes pedagogic practice, including how meanings are made, so important.

Picture books which demand effort from readers offer much to children of all ages. They raise certain issues about reading with particular clarity: the relationship between author and reader, how readers discover what kind of text they are handling, how they need to move back and forth within a text and how endings are anticipated. Such books offer insights into the way texts are structured; for example, that irony emerges as the reader puts words and pictures together. Many picture books require a reading not unlike that of short, complex poems: visual images prompt verbal interpretations, often provoking differences of opinion which can be discussed in small groups. The book is 'out there', away from the pupils, and argument is thus 'safer' or less confrontational; indeed, there is usually a sense of shared exploration, leading to an agreed reading.

Many modern picture books are intellectually sophisticated and may demand a range of experience and developmental understanding that are beyond very young children, while being visually engaging for older children. Upper junior pupils have been immersed in the visual images of the contemporary world for a number of years; picture books can create opportunities for developing literacy, and literary and aesthetic understanding at a level which might not be possible with more dense texts. Fox (1996: 599) believes that the potential value of picture books in the classroom falls 'far short of full realisation' and that the endorsement of picture books in upper primary and secondary schools is more honoured in theory than practice. Teachers of younger children sometimes have such commitment to 'enjoyment' that the idea of studying complex picture books evokes misplaced hostility. So such 'texts' have suffered from a lack of critical exposition and a failure of experts in pedagogy to suggest how they might be best explored.

Goldman's research (in Hunt, 1996: 93) into the function of story in transmitting the rules of conduct and moral conventions and values of society, concludes that 'external perceptions of story require more than simply exposure to the narrative form', implying that the writer-reader relationship needs more guided effort by primary teachers. Even the simplest picture book can be less simple than it appears, and older children should be encouraged to return to this genre once their sense of humour is sufficiently developed. The best picture books are open to interpretation because they leave so much unsaid; coming to terms with the subtext, however, demands serious thought because, although the texts of these books seem straightforward, the meaning behind them is not. Quality of illustrations, too, can excite and challenge older children to think about their own and other people's experiences and reflect on possibilities about characters, events and motives for actions.

Older children are enabled to think more deeply about the issues raised by stimulating visuals and minimal well-chosen text. Brevity of text is one of the most important advantages for older children working with picture books, as it allows a swift comprehension and overview seldom afforded by novels and enables them to discuss the books in, arguably, a more sophisticated and satisfying way. And in a picture book it is easier to make reference to specific elements in support of a specific point. Good picture books can contribute to the development of children's thinking throughout the primary years. When Baddeley and Eddershaw (1994: 75) worked with ten and eleven year olds, they found that pupils made sophisticated literary analyses of picture books and the authors emphasise the potential of picture books to develop such skills.

Throughout Europe over the last 20 years, gifted artists have shown that the picture book is no longer the preserve of very young children, demonstrating its particular ability to catch the irony and the tang of contemporary childhood. In England, writers for the older primary age-range showed signs of interest in new forms of challenging content, combining visual and verbal techniques in a highly original way. Their commercial success proves that children can appreciate sophisticated interplays between writer and reader. Resourceful teachers are helping older readers to become more sophisticated in their understanding of how texts work and of relationships operating in the secondary worlds depicted, by using picture books that are open to interpretation, have more complex stories and are free from a didactic attitude. In future, there will be the opportunity to add another dimension to this teaching, by using the visual narratives of picture books from other European countries.

39

Chapter Five
Compiling the European Picture Book Collection

In the previous chapters I have tried to develop a theoretical rationale for using picture books in upper primary classrooms which would both implement a European dimension and facilitate greater literary and linguistic understanding. This chapter describes a project designed to put the theory into practice and to identify suitable picture books to form a European collection.

At a symposium in Belgium in 1993, designed to encourage its participants to consider the implementation of a European dimension in teacher education, papers described existing projects in various member states that linked to aspects of the European dimension. At the plenary session, delegates new to the concept of such European projects were invited to suggest further ways in which European knowledge and awareness could be facilitated at both primary and secondary levels. The idea of using children's literature was well received. I submitted an outline of how this might be done, together with contact names from educational establishments in the fifteen European member states, and the proposal was approved. After several months of negotiations with the EU, funding was secured.

An initial symposium was held at the IUFM (Institut Universitaire de Formation des Maîtres) in Douai, with experts on children's literature from all fifteen member states of the European Union. Participants presented their views about the development of children's literature in their own countries. Specific focus was to be placed on picture books, with a view to choosing representative examples which could be included in a European picture book collection. The aim was to bring together a collection of books that would meet the objectives of the EU recommendations to implement a European dimension in primary education.

The objectives of the symposium were to:

- bring together specialists on children's literature from all member states

- engage in dialogue which could lead to a greater understanding of children's literature throughout Europe

- facilitate the sharing of children's picture books throughout the member states

- discuss the promotion of a European dimension in education through children's literature

- develop materials which would enable teachers to implement a European dimension in primary classrooms, thus giving children a greater literary, linguistic and cultural awareness.

Because all the potential European participants were to be funded for involvement in the symposium, overall criteria for the papers could be predetermined so that particular themes would be covered. We were interested to know from these experts which picture books were currently popular in their country and which might be selected for inclusion in a European collection.

After several months of communication, one participant from each member state was chosen to present a paper at the Douai Symposium in February 1996, and all agreed to include selected picture books as part of their presentations, details of which can be found in Cotton, 1998.

The papers (Cotton, 1996) outlined the historical development of children's literature in each member state. Sweden, for example, has a long history of children's literature which has influenced other countries considerably, whereas Portugal has only recently begun to develop a cultural literacy in terms of children's picture books, due mainly to the long dictatorship. Politics have affected the development and role of children's literature in many countries. The recent unification of Germany has spawned a new generation of erstwhile East German writers for children who are now influencing the themes and language used in German children's literature. Social and cultural aspects of European life, such as languages, artistic references, geographical locations and customs have also had some effect. Luxembourg is striving to develop a body of children's literature which will reinforce the importance of the Luxembourgish language, while the UK rarely includes books from other European cultures, even in translation.

The content of the picture books discussed in the papers showed some remarkable similarities. Dunbar (Ireland) focused on contemporary universal themes of childhood, which appear to be moving away from the secure home environment of earlier 20th Century stories towards what Kåreland (Sweden) suggested is a world of childhood responsibilities. Perrot (France) discussed the importance of secondary worlds, especially those that relate to the fears and concerns of all children. The relationships between parents and children are often dominant, as are themes of fear and loneliness, as expressed by Forsman (Finland). The influence of authors and illustrators on the development of children's literature in Europe was emphasised by Defourny (Belgium) and Kåreland (Sweden) amongst others. Meek (England) focused on the important role played by writers such as the Ahlbergs in creating a world which reflects the 'Englishness of the English' yet travels well – their work is widely acknowledged throughout Europe. Illustrations, too, have a part to play, and Spain's contribution focused on illustrations, specifically the references to Dali and Velazquez in one picture book. Other contributors also referred to visual intertextual pictures.

Each participant identified picture books which they felt were particularly relevant to promoting cultural identity and a love of reading. Only Meek (England), supported by Hill (Scotland) and Marriott (N. Ireland), stressed the importance of the books themselves in facilitating the reading process. This appears to be a uniquely UK theme, although the French participant did point out the importance of the rolling biscuit in *Roule Gallette* (see Cotton, 1996) which moves from left to right, hence guiding the young reader in the reading direction. Participants from Sweden, Finland, Italy and Luxembourg acknowledged that their countries do now appear to be focusing more on the idea of the importance of the book itself to the reading process. Certainly all participants were aware of the central role that picture books have in the enjoyment of reading and learning about other cultures, so all were able to contribute to and help select picture books for the European Picture Book Collection (EPBC).

The concluding discussions focused on the final choice of picture books for a European collection and it was agreed that the EPBC should be based upon the following rationale:

- it should comprise one picture book from each country and reflect a universal childhood theme

- where possible, this should be within a specific cultural setting

- the priority should be from the viewpoint of the child and the experiences of childhood that countries have in common, rather than what separates them

- each book should tell a visual story and be accompanied by minimal text

- each book should have an accompanying cassette in the original language, to help children become aware of the linguistic diversity within the European Union

- a short rationale for choosing each book should be provided, plus a translation or re-telling of the story in English, and three ideas for teachers to use the books in school.

The European Picture Book Collection now comprises the books listed in Table 1, one from each of the fifteen member states, with the exception of one each for England, Scotland, N. Ireland and Wales and two from Belgium, one in French and one in Flemish. The final choice was made because each book:

- is considered amongst the very best from that country

- is used widely in primary schools

- depicts a universal childhood theme

- tells a visual story

- reflects the culture of that country, where possible.

It was suggested that the EPBC should be up-dated bi-annually in order to keep abreast of contemporary picture books in each member state.

After the symposium, all participants were asked to supply a brief rationale for their final choice of book for the EPBC. An overview of the responses is set out in Table 2.

Finally, the symposium participants were asked to provide three things that would help with developing the materials for use in school:

44

- a short, written summary of the contents of each book in English

- a cassette of the story in its original language and

- three ideas of how the books might be used with upper primary children.

The EPBC was used by teachers in six UK schools during 1997. Four teachers from each school volunteered to use the books for one month with their upper primary classes (10-11 year olds). All wanted the children to learn more about their European neighbours. Some of the teachers spoke languages other than English and had spent time in other parts of Europe, but many were interested in learning more about Europe for themselves.

The UK pilot revealed the following:

- all the teachers involved felt that they themselves had learned a great deal about both Europe and picture books

- they were surprised how little their pupils knew about Europe **before the project**

- they were amazed by how much they knew **after the project**

- the children were fascinated by the books and the languages

Table 1: The European Picture Book Collection

Country	Language	Book	Author/Illustrator
Austria	German	*Das Land der Ecken*	Irene Ulitzka and Gerhard Gepp
Belgium	Flemish	*Lotje is jarig*	Lieve Baeten
Belgium	French	*Un jour mon Prince viendra*	Andréa Nève and Kitty Crowther
Denmark	Danish	*Mosekonens Bryg*	Ib Spang Olsen
Finland	Swedish	*VEM ska trösta knyttet?*	Tove Jansson
France	French	*Une nuit, un chat ...*	Yvan Pommaux
Germany	German	*Hallo, kleiner Wal*	Gisela Kalow and Achim Bröger
Greece	Greek	*The story-spinner meets the sugar-wizard*	A. Kyritsopoulus
Ireland	Gaelic	*Naomh Pádraig agus Crom Dubh*	Gabriel Rosenstock
Italy	Italian	*La bambina che non voleva andare a dormire*	Pinin Carpi
Luxembourg	Luxembourgish; French; German	*D'Grisette an D'Choupette um motorrad*	Anne-Marie Theis and Mariette Ries
Netherlands	Dutch	*Kees en Keetje*	Jantien Buisman
Portugal	Portuguese	*A ovelha negra*	Cristina Malaquias
Spain	Spanish	*El guardián del olvido*	Joan Manuel Gisbert and Alfonso Ruano
Sweden	Swedish	*Kan du vissla Johanna*	Ulf Stark and Anna Höglund
England	English	*Starting School*	Janet and Allan Ahlberg
N. Ireland	English	*War and Peas*	Michael Foreman
Scotland	English	*Katie Morag and the new pier*	Mairi Hedderwick
Wales	Welsh	*Cantre'r Gwaelod*	Siân Lewis and Jackie Morris

45

Table 2: Rationale for Choosing Each Book

Country	Rationale for Choice of Book
Austria	Example of possible harmony within differences that exist between countries
Belgium (Flemish)	Reflects the cosiness of Flemish homes
Belgium (French)	Addresses the theme of 'witches' common in Belgian books
Denmark	Engagement of fantasy and feeling from a Danish point of view
Finland	Well known Finnish author; addresses theme of loneliness and shyness
France	Popular French author; theme of growing up and going out alone
Germany	Universal theme: friendship between adults and animals
Greece	A Greek fantasy tale, tinged with elements of reality – 'having too much of a good thing'
Ireland	An Irish folktale which involves elements of culture and manners
Italy	An Italian tale of a little girl who wants to hear stories rather than go to bed
Luxembourg	A Luxembourgish story which reflects the diversity of languages used in this country
Netherlands	A tale of friendship and losing it; reflecting aspects of Dutch culture
Portugal	Quality of illustrations; link between imagery, animism and fantasy
Spain	Reflects light and shade of Spanish life; visual intertextuality
Sweden	Children's unconventional ways of solving problems, in a Swedish setting
England	Relates to the world of school as seen through the eyes of children
N. Ireland	Moral tale about the relationship between a rich country and a poor one
Scotland	The theme of 'change', where the child is supportive, within a Scottish setting
Wales	Well-loved Welsh story which has echoes of other cultures

- many parents who had mainland European origins became involved in the project, which helped those with little English to be more involved with the school

- although the books were mainly used with 10 and 11 year olds, teachers of younger children also found the books useful

- all the teachers felt that the materials could provide the basis for a year's work in school

- more guidance was wanted on how to use the EPBC, resource book and cassettes.

The European Committee of the International Reading Association gave the EPBC the *Innovative Reading Promotion in Europe* award for 1996/7.

The second symposium, designed to re-unite colleagues from the EU member states to discuss the progress of the project, was held at the Austrian Study Centre for Peace and Conflict Resolution in May, 1998. The Federal Ministry of Education and Cultural Affairs offered to host this symposium, as it was felt that the project would enhance Austria's standing within the European Community. The Austrian book selected for inclusion in the EPBC, *Das Land der Ecken* (*The land of corners*), was chosen because it has a truly European theme and presents an example of possible harmony despite the differences that exist between countries.

47

What began as a project to develop materials for use in primary schools within the member states of the European Union now appears to be developing into a trans-European project. Holding this symposium in Austria meant that many Central European nations could participate, due to their proximity and to funding from the Austrian government. The papers presented by colleagues from Bosnia-Herzegovina, Bulgaria, Croatia, Czech Republic, Estonia, Hungary, Poland, Romania, Slovak Republic and Slovenia made a startling impact on the proceedings. The dramatic contrast in materials available and attitudes towards picture books and learning to read, between these countries and the fifteen member states, can be seen in the second set of papers (Cotton, 1998).

Virtually all the contributions were concerned with how visual texts can enhance children's reading development and knowledge of literary forms. Participants emphasized the need to share expertise across nations so as to facilitate a European dimension in primary education and create a greater cultural awareness and understanding. Since the first trials of the EPBC in the UK in 1997, the collection has also been used in Finnish primary schools (1998) and the process continued in other EU countries in 1999 and 2000. An evaluation of the Finnish trials can be found in Cotton, 1998.

The EPBC books used in the trials all have minimal texts, in the original languages, and are accompanied by a cassette or CD of the story told in the same language. The translations, together with activities for use in school, have been collated into a teachers' resource book and form the basis of a training package. The books all relate to universal childhood themes and allow, through the visual narratives, a recognition of those aspects of 'Europeaness' with which all children can identify. Alongside the visual texts, teachers and pupils can listen also to the languages of the books and begin to learn a little about the commonalities of language. It is hoped that this will alleviate the anxieties many children may have about language learning.

The materials are being developed for in-service teacher training courses throughout Europe, and adapted to comply with each national government's documentation. Thanks to the heavy involvement of the Austrian ministry and the participation of so many Central European countries, the third meeting, funded by the EU, was hosted by the Chair of Education at Eötvös University, Budapest, Hungary in May 2000, where the on-going research findings were presented.

48

Chapter Six
A Framework for Analysing European Picture Books

T he results of the EPBC trials in UK schools indicated that many of the teachers required more guidance on how to use the materials in school, especially to help children understand the visual narratives of these picture book texts. So I decided to create a method for teachers to analyse the books before using them. Chapter Six describes the semiotic text analysis framework (STA) which I developed for the nineteen books in the European Picture Book Collection (EPBC), and suggests how these books might facilitate a European dimension in primary education.

All discussion of texts in this chapter refers to the visual narratives presented in the EPBC. Each of the nineteen books has been selected because it represents a universal childhood theme by means of a coherent visual narrative story-line. Although each picture in each book is accompanied by a small amount of text, visual attributes must be the primary focus, since upper primary children in each member state will not understand the languages of all the books. Once the beliefs and values underlying the texts as well as the characterisation, setting and plot are understood, linguistic links can be made and the polysemic nature of the texts put to use in primary classrooms.

Each text is set within an evaluative framework which discusses the visual narratives that can be offered to young European readers who, through these European picture books, are likely to learn more about children in other member states, their cultures, stories and interests. I suggest that the children have more in common, because of their childhood, than they differ because of culture. The framework for analysis has its roots in semiotics. It provides a means of eliciting the thematic universality of European picture books and their relevance for study in upper primary classrooms. I believe that this approach makes it possible to focus on the visual narratives of picture book texts and discuss the ability of each to communicate empathy and understanding.

The discipline of semiotics, the study of signs, was developed by Barthes (1957) when building on the ideas of Saussure (1916) and Pierce (1931). Barthes (1957: 110/11) believes that pictures become a kind of writing as soon as they are meaningful and, like writing, are an aspect of language which requires a lexis. He takes language to mean any significant sign, whether verbal or visual, and suggests that 'a picture will be a kind of speech for us in the same way as a newspaper article; even objects will become speech, if they mean something'. Together with a number of other Europeans he uses the linguistic sign to analyse social symbols. Everything non-linguistic – images, objects, bodily stance – is treated as if it were a language. Eco (1979) endorses this thinking, for him semiotics studies all cultural processes as 'processes of communication', and he defines the communicative process as 'the passage of a signal from a source through a transmitter, along a channel to a destination'.

Blonsky (1985: 150) suggests that, through these signs, 'we can grasp the culture's bloodstream', and supports Eco's belief that culture can be fully studied according to its semiotic profile. Consequently, I have chosen a semiotic analysis for the picture book texts which builds on concepts developed by theorists working in picture book analysis. The theoretical rationale underpinning the thematic framework is made up of:

- a universal theme (Douai Symposium, 1996)

- a classification of picture books (Graham, 1990): People, Setting, Story

50
- four interrelated categories:

    - visual codes (Moebius, 1986; Nodelman; 1988; Doonan, 1993)

    - visual narrative techniques (Velders, 1992; Thomas, 1994; Bromley, 1996)

    - types of picture book (Lewis, 1994)

    - picture book ingredients (Cotton, 1997, Chapter Four)

Each category contributes to the semiotic text analysis set out in Table 3 and is explained in the following sections. This STA presents the visual ingredients which make the picture book narrative immediately accessible to European children, regardless of their first language. It provides a structure whereby texts can be analysed as materials for discourse, which enables the mimetic (imitatory) function of messages to go back and forth between picture book and reader. In other words, the framework helps pupils to interpret, discuss and evaluate visual imitations of fantasy and reality.

Items in this analytical framework are now explained in more detail.

Table 3 : The STA Framework

THEME

Classification of Picture Books	Category 1 Visual Codes	Category 2 Visual narrative techniques	Category 3 Types of picture book	Category 4 Picture book ingredients
				How the picture book works
	Position	Distance	Boundary breaking	
People				Semiotics
	Size	Place		
	Perspective			Ideology
		Level		
	Frame		Excess	Metafiction
	Line	Time		
Setting	Colour			Intertextuality
	Shape	Cartoon format		The concept of childhood
	Action	Trigger images	Indeterminancy	
	Movement			Secondary/possible words
		Use of icons		
Story	Facial expressions			Fantasy/reality
	Body gestures	Circumstantial details	Parody	
	Cinematic devices			Universal childhood themes
		Expressions of emotion		
				Characterisation
			Performance	Relationships

51

Universal childhood theme

The universal childhood theme of *friendship* was chosen for the EPBC, after being identified at the Douai symposium as a potentially unifying element. Peter Schneck (see Chapter Five) suggested that with so many conflicting European issues, it was important to help children in member states to empathise with each other through friendship themes. His Austrian choice, *Das Land der Ecken*, explores how two children from very different worlds become friends.

Friendship can be represented in picture books more broadly and more profoundly than is normally experienced in reality. Some of the stories in the EPBC locate readers in situations which allow self-reflection; others convey messages which concern human issues. Their special visual accessibility has the potential to give children early encounters with literary texts that will prepare them for their later literary and real lives. Humanity's concerns are discussed that are ageless and universal: growing up, facing change, separating from parents, developing a sense of being one's own person, becoming aware of social expectations and personal responsibilities. Many children experience disruptive emotions like fear and anxiety from a very young age. It is through the kinds of everyday experiences represented in certain of the stories in the EPBC that children's learning and understanding of the real world may be facilitated.

52

Classification of picture books

Three of Graham's (1990) picture book headings have been adopted to classify the EPBC texts, so providing a focused analysis of one narrative element in each book. *People, setting* and *story*, are major elements in any narrative, and in depth picture book analysis is likely to facilitate a number of literary competences (see Chapter Eight). Each book in the EPBC has been assigned to the most appropriate classification and a rationale given. For example, the visual characterisation of the protagonist in *VEM ska trösta knyttet?* from Finland (Chapter Seven: fig.3), changes and develops throughout the book; the setting of *Kan du vissla Johanna?* (Chapter Seven: fig.8) visually reflects certain facets of Swedish life; and *Kees en Keetje*, from the Netherlands (Chapter Seven: fig.14), presents a clear and well set out visual narrative storyline. The picture books in the EPBC have been classified as follows:

People: *VEM ska trösta knyttet?* (Finland)
       Une nuit, un chat... (France)
       La bambina che non voleva andare a dormire (Italy)
       Un jour mon prince viendra (Belgium – French)
       Lotje is jarig (Belgium – Flemish)

Setting: *Kan du vissla Johanna* (Sweden)
  Katie Morag and the new pier (Scotland)
  El guardián del olvido (Spain)
  Mosekonens Bryg (Denmark)
  Naomh Pádraig agus Crom Dubh (Ireland)
  Cantre'r Gwaelod (Wales)

Story: *Kees en Keetje* (Netherlands)
  War and Peas (Northern Ireland)
  The story-spinner meets the sugar-wizard (Greece)
  Hallo, kleiner Wal (Germany)
  D'Grisette an D'Choupette um motorrad (Luxembourg)
  Das land der Ecken (Austria)
  A olvelha negra (Portugal)
  Starting School (England)

People

The picture book is one of the first places where young children encounter fictional characters and where, suggests Graham (1990: 27), convincing portraits are given by creative illustrators. Children can read the pictures much as they interpret behaviour in real life. As their learning progresses and they begin to read the visual world around them, they can take on more complex issues and begin to understand how texts work and how characters develop and respond to each other. Children with a firm grounding in their own culture then become ready to move further afield and familiarise themselves through literature with the childhood worlds of other countries. This is not always easy, because there is so little accessible material in the UK in other languages, especially European, and there are the problems of translation (see Chapter Three).

53

Children must attend to the individuality of the people in stories so that they become involved with the characters and want to know what happens to them next. Graham (1990: 41) suggests that involvement with characters can be taught through 'good illustrations', referring to three books by Gabrielle Vincent of France and to books by Dick Bruna (Netherlands), Hergé (Belgium), and Roberto Innocenti (Italy). She comments on 'a splendid Parisian busker's broad black hat and flamboyant yellow scarf' (1990: 41) but is not concerned to make specific cultural references or discuss the origins of the stories. So she misses further evidence that certain layers of meaning are only accessible through the illustrations.

Setting

Meaning is also conveyed through the settings in which stories take place, and this is especially true of picture books. Just as writers have various ways of creating a backdrop for their stories, so illustrators may with line, shape or colour suggest a lonely room or an enchanted garden. With deft under-statement or by providing a wealth of detail, they enable readers to enter into secondary worlds. When detail is lacking, suggests Graham (1990: 65/6), 'we have the opportunity to fill in, to authenticate a setting; when detail is abundant we can select with discretion, recognise with delight or learn with interest'. If, however, there are contradictions within the visuals, as with the setting of *El guardián del olvido* (Chapter Seven: fig.10) reality and fantasy worlds combine. Through the illustrator's use of colour and light, the mood created facilitates a deeper understanding of the quest that the young prota-gonist is undertaking.

Story

A visual story is a sequence of pictures which demands that readers can see relationships between objects and draw inferences. According to Graham (1990: 67), children learn essential narrative structures, story shape and story schemata from pictures which both teach and demand 'literary literacy'. Wells (1985: 96) observes that this literary knowledge enables readers to follow and construct narrative and expository sequences, recognise causes, anticipate consequences and consider the motives and emotions that are inextricably bound up with every human action.

Part of the act of reading is knowing that the early stages of a story require readers to tolerate uncertainty. We are confronted by narrative techniques that establish links between things we find difficult to connect so we are forced to reconsider data we at first thought to be quite straightforward (Iser, 1978: 68). Stories have an overall structure: in the beginning anything is possible; in the middle things become more probable; in the ending everything is necessary (Goodman, 1954: 102).

In books with minimal or no text, the bones of narrative are more apparent. As texts become longer, illustrations may be used less to tell a continuous story and more to guide readers' grasp of significant points in the plot, while also creating character, setting and story-line. Although there are visual conventions that have to be learned, pictures are often culturally specific, so visual readings are not always straightforward. Pictures can be understood from a remarkably early age, as wordless picture books demonstrate (Knudsen Lindauer, 1988; Keiffer, 1995). These enable illustrators to display a range of story-events which add to readers' growing command and under-standing of narrative.

Category I: Visual codes

Visual codes are in the readings of *people, setting* and *story* within picture book narratives. The structure for this category has been based on the work of Moebius (1986), Nodelman (1988) and Doonan (1993).

Positioning and size

The positioning and size of a character on a page is often significant – is it high or low, right, left or in the centre of the page? Height might be a mark of social status or power, or of positive self image, whereas a low position may denote low spirits or an unfavourable social status (Moebius, 1986). Characters can be strengthened or weakened depending on whether the character is centred or in the margins, in close-up or long-shot (ie large or small). The more often a character is depicted on the same or facing pages, the more likely that it is in a position of control; rather like Anna in *La bambina che non voleva andare a dormire* (Chapter Seven: fig.5). A character that is on the margin, or near the bottom of the page, is likely to be more disadvantaged than one in the centre; whilst one shown on the left of the page is likely to be seen as more secure than one on the right, where a thought is usually completed. And excessively large characters could be a visual feature of an overblown ego, as in the characterisation of the fat king in *War and Peas* or the witch in *Un jour mon Prince viendra*. This power and influence, exhibited by many of the central characters in the EPBC texts, is discussed further in Chapter Seven.

55

Perspective

Perspective is a graphic technique which creates the impression of depth and three dimensions on a two dimensional surface (Doonan, 1993: 86). It allows readers to follow the presence or absence of horizontals, vanishing points and contrasts between façades and backgrounds (Moebius, 1986). The sudden absence of a horizon may well spell danger, or open space above it leads the reader to question what lies beyond. A character depicted in two dimensions, such as the matron of the old people's home in *Kan du vissla Johanna*, is likely to be less open-minded or capable of imaginative scope than a character given three-dimensional depth, like the enigmatic guardian of lost things in *El guardián del olvido* (Chapter Seven: fig.10).

Frame

A frame surrounds picture book visuals and can strongly affect the inter-pretations readers make of a visual text. A picture smaller than the page on which it appears is said to be framed by the white margins of the paper that surrounds it; Doonan (1993:84) calls this an air frame but there are several types of frames. Pictures can also be framed by decorative boarders containing complementary images like, for example, the clouds in *A ovelha negra* (Chapter Seven: fig.20). A rigid frame contains events but if the frame is broken, as in D'Grisette an *D'Choupette um motorrad* (Chapter Seven: fig.18), empowerment of the central character is intensified. On the other hand, as in *Lotje is jarig* (Chapter Seven: fig.7), a free-hand drawn line framing the picture appears less formal and allows for a livelier effect – as if the frame itself is breathing the pictured events to life (Doonan, 1993: 84),

A frame also enables the reader to identify with the worlds both inside and outside of the story (Moebius, 1986). A framed illustration provides a limited glimpse into a world, whereas an unframed picture constitutes a total experience, a view from within. The frame usually marks a limit beyond which the text cannot go, or from which the image cannot escape – as with the young boy in *VEM ska trösta knyttet?* (Chapter Seven: fig.3). Breaking the frame is likely to signify the forbidden or miraculous. Characters are likely to be more secure and content in a circular frame than in a rectangular one, which often suggests a problem. Both devices are used in *Kan du vissla Johanna* where Grandfather is shown free with the children yet contained by the nursing home.

A picture book provides a temporal as well as a spatial frame: it has an opening and a closing page, a cover with two sides. What the front and back pages say is generally complementary and symmetrical. The heart of the book lies somewhere in the middle of this outer frame. This particularly applies to *Das Land der Ecken*, where the angular and circular endpapers at the front and back of the book signify the change in attitude that has taken place during the course of the story – a movement from egocentricity to an acceptance of difference.

Line

The intensity of a character's experience may be represented by the thickness or thinness of lines, by their smoothness or jaggedness, by their profusion or spareness, and by whether they run parallel or at sharp angles to each other (Moebius, 1986). Spare lines may suggest mobility and speed, whereas thick, blurred ones tend to denote a comfortable status. Jagged lines and those at sharp angles usually accompany troubled emotions or endangered life, as in *Une nuit, un chat...* while squiggles often signify vitality or a surfeit of energy.

Colour and shape

Apart from the traditional associations of certain colours with certain moods, readers need to be sensitive to colour as a linkage among different objects (Moebius, 1986). Colour and shape often combine to create visual ideas and, according to Nodelman (1988), we associate certain emotions with certain shapes. Squares and rectangles tend to be seen as stable, fixed and rigid whereas rounded shapes appear more comfortable and accommodating, as in *Das Land der Ecken* (Chapter Seven: fig.19).

Action and movement

Many features of visual narrative can be evoked through action and movement: the passing of time for example or causes, effects or intentions. Hodge and Kress (1988: 27) suggest that pictures with 'high modality' (close fit between sign and meaning) tend to be far more static and immobile than those with 'low modality' which avoid realism and lean towards simplicity. Individual pictures can not only depict objects and people but can convey motion – running, jumping, skipping etc. through the position of legs and arms, speed marks and direction lines. And some illustrators use cartoon format to show movement across the page, as in representations of the approaching army in *War and Peas* (Chapter Seven: fig.15).

Facial expressions and body gestures

Other picture book elements such as facial expressions and body gestures denote emotion and relationships between characters. The shape of the eyes and the curve of the mouth in the whale's face in *Hallo, kleiner Wal* (Chapter Seven: fig.17), for example, suggest that this creature is indeed friendly, even though he is towering above his minute human friends. In contrast, the rigid body gestures of Marguerite, the witch in *Un jour mon Prince viendra* (Chapter Seven: fig.6), exhibit total hostility. Many of these visual signs are universally understood but occasionally facial expression and body gestures which are culturally bound can introduce young readers to a new perception. The physical movements and facial contortions of the old woman of the marsh, as she brews her beer to welcome the Danish Spring in *Mosekonens Bryg*, would be incomprehensible to English children without some explanation.

57

Body gestures can be suggested through an indication of direction and movement. Marguerite in *Un jour mon Prince viendra* perfectly illustrates how a character can be projected upwards into a position of power to show aggression. Similarly, the physical gestures of father and son as they move towards each other in *Cantre'r Gwaelod* (Chapter Seven: fig.13) intimate possible conflict. The power of gesture is used to great effect by picture book artists. Characters not looking at each other, for example, depict sadness. Body language is important in supporting the meaning that readers get from a text and particularly so when children are trying to determine the relationship between one character and another; a solitary figure in a particular pose would be difficult to understand unless portrayed within the wider context of the story. It is the ability to read gestures as well as facial expressions that enables interpretation of a visual narrative text. In *Kees en Keetje* (Chapter Seven: fig.14), for example, the hostile back to back positioning of the two main characters immediately denotes disharmony.

Cinematic devices

Cinematic devices are readily used in picture books, such as the 'establishing shot' used at the beginning of stories to set the scene (Nodelman, 1988). The endpapers at the beginning and end of the book are rather like the filmic device of pre and post credits, where the author/director allows a preview or extension of the actual story. Picture book illustrators sometimes make use of 'cutting' to link two pictures together, the dominant shape from the first picture being reflected in the next. Even more common is cinematic framing where the shape and size of the image is altered by the closing frame. Picture book illustrators tend mostly to use mid-shots and long shots at eye level (Nodelman, 1988). Very recent picture books are exploiting a wide variety of cinematic devices: *El guardián del olvido* uses a sequence of close-ups to create the opening episode of the book, as well as simultaneous action through 'split-screens'.

Category 2: Visual narrative techniques

Visual narrative techniques suggested by Velders (1992) work alongside the visual codes just discussed, adding further dimensions to the reading of picture books. In addition, the artistic techniques discussed by Thomas (1994) and their practical application outlined by Bromley (1996) contribute to the structure for Category 3 of the STA. Like the codes, they too can facilitate children's understanding of people, setting and story.

Distance, place, level and time

Velders (1992: 26) maintains that personal involvement with the image depends on four visual narrative techniques, for which he has developed an analytic framework based on:

- *Distance* – a long distance view increases concern and decreases the narrative character, as in *El guardián del olvido* (Chapter Seven: fig.10); a close-up shows the reverse, as demonstrated by Toffle *VEM ska trösta knyttet?* (Chapter Seven: fig.3).

- *Place* – the positioning behind a person or act evokes identification with it, again exemplified by Toffle; positioning facing a person or act evokes confrontation, as can be seen by father and son in *Cantre'r Gwaelod* (Chapter Seven: fig.13).

- *Level* – a viewpoint from above or below a person or object evokes emotions of superiority or dread. The Fat King in *War and Peas* views the diminutive Lion King from on high, overpowering him visually (Chapter Seven: fig.15).

- *Time* – depicted through sequences of images or montage of shots, as in *Kees en Keetje* (Chapter Seven: fig.14) with the possibility of 'flash back' or 'flash forward'.

Cartoon format

Wordless picture books often use a cartoon format. This narrative element is crucial to the choice of texts for the EPBC as children will be required to read the visuals before the written text. *Hallo, kleiner Wal* (Chapter Seven: fig.17) and *The story-spinner meets the sugar-wizard* (Chapter Seven: fig.16) both use this to good effect, particularly in story sequencing and character development.

Trigger images

Picture book texts also contain trigger images which activate response to the whole narrative (Thomas, 1994). Children use these signs and symbols to identify themes they know or familiar situations. The spinning top on the fourth verso page of *El guardián del olvido*, for example, at first enables readers to identify with the childhood character and then leads them into the story.

Icons

Closely linked to the trigger image is the use of icons (Bromley, 1996). Iconography is the technique where signs, symbols and colour are employed to identify individual figures and situations. Identification of icons encourages children to construct and test hypotheses about a narrative, as in the case of St Patrick in *Naomh Pádraig agus Crom Dubh* (Chapter Seven: fig.12) where the images of the saint's heavenly halo and the cross on his mitre enable links to be made with the essence of the story, particularly for Christians.

Circumstantial details

Circumstantial details, which do not carry the story on their own but may provide important support (Thomas, 1994), encourage readers to scan the pages looking for clues and read each page several times because the pictures are full of informative images. It is circumstantial detail that draws children back into the books over and over again; the pictures seem to be constructed so that they will not notice every detail at once but will go back time and time again. The toy car on the first recto page of *Une nuit, un chat...*, for example, draws the reader's eye to small details which add to both character and setting as well as to the story.

Expressions of emotion

Expressions of emotion created through subtle nuances of detail, like using light and colour to capture mood, can greatly enhance visual narratives and children become successful at reading pictures which depict emotion through colour. The lighting of scenes to reflect the changes of the characters' moods, not unlike film techniques, are important contributory factors in picture book narratives. Bright colours are associated with exhilaration and discovery, dark colours with disappointment and confusion. Dark or sombre colours also mean gloom and despondency; as in the greyness of the pictures surrounding the miserable Granny Island in *Katie Morag and the new pier*, whereas the bright yellows and blues encircling the happy young witch in *Lotje is jarig* indicate joy.

Category 3: Types of picture book

In Lewis' taxonomy (1994: 29) he matches the unique features of the metafictive picture book with prose fiction. Metafiction draws attention to the ways in which both fictional and real worlds are constructed through language, and there could be types of picture book which exemplify the metafictive. Despite the differences between prose text and the picture book, the kinds of rules that get broken are remarkably similar so that focus on the possible metafictive elements within the EPBC texts may well facilitate an understanding of the techniques used by writers and illustrators of European picture books, and prepare children for the novels they might read later in their school careers.

Category 3 of the STA applies aspects of Lewis' metafictive taxonomy to the EPBC, trying to extend his thinking in relation to a wider body of picture book texts. An important feature of the metafictive picture book is the interaction between picture and written text; a visual analysis is not always sufficient to understand this form fully. The importance of the written text is discussed where appropriate, particularly as the metafictive, according to Lewis, would seem to make a difference to learning to read (1994: 42). His five metafictive strategies are now discussed:

Boundary breaking

In this type of picture book the central characters have the ability to influence the story's development, usually stepping beyond the boundaries of the story itself. They often address readers directly at the beginning of the story or create new characters or even affect the direction of the story. In *Zoem, de zebra*, mentioned in Chapter Four, the interaction of the animal with the storybook's illustrator results in a dialogue which creates the narrative story-line, thus moving away from conventional storytelling techniques. In the EPBC book from Portugal's *A ovelha negra*, too, the author discusses her own visual perceptions of cloud formations and invites readers both to inter-act and to decide the outcome of the story.

Excess

Excess, suggests, Lewis (1994: 30) is a common metafictive strategy used in picture books, by which the incredible becomes plausible. Many picture books have an 'over the top quality' and frequently test literary norms. Thresholds are dissolved and decorum ignored. The unthinkable or the unmentionable can happen; the imagery becomes increasingly extravagant, going well beyond the bounds of realism, as in *Hello kleiner Wal* (Chapter Seven: fig.17) where the relationship between an elderly couple and a young whale leads to the old people helping to rear her offspring.

Indeterminacy

Indeterminacy is the opposite of excess, in that the reader is provided with too little information. Lewis (1994:32) suggests that all stories are built upon absence. This is not unlike cinematic conventions, where directors cut from one scene to another without too much explanation. Some picture books expose the gaps and reveal the comic absurdity of a situation; offering no explicit authorisation for a specific interpretation, allowing readers to derive their own meanings. This may be achieved through the juxtaposition of fantasy with reality. *Das Land der Ecken* is a fantasy land of corners where other shapes are forbidden. Through a series of quite unconnected visuals, a young child is seen trying to cope with the entry of an alien object into his world. The parallel with reality is acceptance of difference, but it is only through considering what is missing from the visual narrative that individual readings are possible.

Parody

Picture book creators are adept at parodic transformations, where the aim is not to ridicule any particular author or style but to make the book into a joke by sending up conventions (Lewis, 1994: 35). Parody is always subversive, refusing to accept that which is culturally determined. The problem in rela-tion to European picture books is for children to understand cross-cultural mores. Parody based on European folktale heritage such as *Un jour mon Prince viendra* is likely to be more widely acceptable than *War and Peas* which is more firmly based in one culture. The parodic features in these texts are further discussed in Chapter Eight.

61

Performance

Many picture books are interactive and participatory and the makers of 'pop-ups' or 'movables' generally seem to be more concerned with the picture book as object rather than the book as fiction (Lewis, 1994: 39). What movables share with the metafictive is a disrespect for rules and conventions and they seem to assume a willingness on the part of their audience to engage in the forms of play they offer. So even though many movables are 'nothing more than a cynical exploitation of the propensity of the young to engage in forms of play', the phenomenon needs careful attention.

At the Douai symposium that preceded the EPBC, two of the presentations focused on the role movables can play in understanding visual narratives. Geoff Fox suggested how movable books might be considered more analytically, without losing sight of the young readers. For movables to be true facilitators of the reading process there need to be interactive devices which 'are necessary for the plot to move forward'. Perrot pointed out that movable picture books allow children to enter a world full of 'literary surprises' and this initiates them into 'cultural conventions and proficiency in intellectual autonomy' (Cotton, 1996: vii). So the performance aspect of the metafictive picture book now seems to be taken seriously.

Category 4: Picture book ingredients

The preceding categories have all influenced the theoretical perspectives presented in Chapter Four. Category 4 of the STA framework summarises these and identifies the picture book 'ingredients' which facilitate universal readings of texts and work on a number of levels for older readers. The hallmark of good picture books is that they invite response at the symbolic level, are open to interpretation and can be significant in the socialisation of children into the ideology of our culture. Writers and illustrators deliberately exploit the 'metafictive' nature of picture books, and include visual intertextual clues which can also be used heuristically in discussion of other cultures.

Universal themes of childhood are discerned in picture books where the illustrations serve as obvious and covert socialising processes of childhood and contemporary constructions of childhood. Picture book texts present many possible worlds inhabited by diverse kinds of characters, and challenge the readers by blending realistic and fantastic elements in everyday settings. The magical property of books is universal, and the fact that different cultures have stories in which the same elements appear indicates that certain themes have basic human appeal. The nature of the social world depicted in picture books can be determined by the types of characters that appear most frequently, portrayed within specific social relationships. Thus the EPBC books have the potential to develop visual learning strategies related to the universal childhood themes which are highlighted in Table 4.

Table 4: Thematic Picture Book Ingredients within the EPBC

Country	Concept of Childhood and Universal Themes	Secondary and Possible Worlds: Fantasy v. Reality	Characters and Relationships	Power of Pictures and Cultural References
A. CHARACTER:				
VEM ska trösta knyttet? (Finland)	loneliness/being shy/finding a friend	a real situation set within a fantasy world	lonely child to child relationship	pictures contrast with the darkness of Finland
Une nuit, un chat... (France)	growing up/a child's first adventure	real situation set within a fantasy world of animals	protective parent to child relationship	colours/clothes/architecture – French style
La Bambina... (Italy)	the joy of bedtime stories	a real life setting with universal references	child trying to control adult	visually refers to Italian lifestyle
Un jour mon Prince viendra (Belgium)	friendship/fear	Parodic fantasy world	romance between two 'adults'	visual power
Lotje is jarig (Belgium)	birthdays/friends/magic	real child in magical fantasy world	caring adults for child and cat	warmth of colour/cosy Flemish homes
B. SETTING:				
Kan du vissla Johanna (Sweden)	family ties/life/death/role of grandparents	a real situation	two children's relationships with adoptive grandad	Swedish setting/links with death
Katie Morag (Scotland)	Change	real experiences	child helping her grandmother	visually refers to Scottish Isles
El guardián del olvido (Spain)	losing things/being lonely/friendship	reality which moves into fantasy	two lost children find friendship	visually refers to Spanish art/artists
Mosekonens Bryg (Denmark)	the coming of Spring	total fantasy to explain reality	family of troll-like characters	Danish folklore/landscape
Naomh Pádraig agus Crom Dubh (Ireland)	customs and manners	a fantasy depiction of folkloric reality	child helps two adults	visually reflects an aspect of Irish folklore
Cantre'r Gwaelod (Wales)	Pride comes before a fall	folk-tale fantasy	father and son relationship	pictures reflect Celtic folk-tale
C. STORY				
Kees en Keetje (Netherlands)	breaking up with friends and making up	real situation as seen by two animals	two animals explore their friendship	pictures depict a Dutch setting; focus on food
War and Peas (N. Ireland)	poverty v. greed/poor v. rich countries	fantasy setting/reality undertones	adult conflict	parallels with country's problems
The story-spinner meets the sugar-wizard (Greece)	having too much of a good thing	fantasy which relates to human desires	adults in a children's world	visually refers to Greek landscape
Hallo, kleiner Wal (Germany)	an unlikely friendship	a fantasy set in real life situation	adults' relationship with animal	friendly dominance of visuals
D'Grisette... (Luxembourg)	being naughty	real life story seen thro' animals' eyes	conflict between children and adults	linguistic cultural references
Das Land der Ecken (Austria)	accepting difference/making friends	everyday problems set in fantasy world	Disharmony between adults and children	focus on shapes
A ovelha negra (Portugal)	coping with difference	fantasy situation related to real life	how animals cope with a stranger	Portuguese countryside
Starting School (England)	starting school	real experiences	8 children + parents	English schools

Under the umbrella theme of *friendship* a number of sub-themes permeate the collection: growing up, family relationships, celebrations and change occur repeatedly, a substantiation and exemplification of ideas expressed in Category 4. Many of the secondary worlds represented stem from real life situations set within a fantasy world, and these often include animals used in an anthropomorphic way to mirror children's own behaviour. But the majority of the relationships between the characters tend to centre around child/child and child/adult interactions, many of them depicted visually through contrasts in colour, shape and imagery representative of the book's country of origin. The treatment of the friendship theme in individual texts is quite distinct, however; each country approaches the concept from a slightly different angle, using a variety of narrative techniques and visual codes.

The semiotic text analysis was created for the EPBC to enable classification of the diverse aspects of visual narratives which appear to facilitate universal understanding, so it has a predominantly visual focus. It could certainly be applied to other book collections, and my general STA framework – which is applied to each of the EPBC books in Chapter Seven – can be used for a similar analysis of other texts.

Chapter Seven
Analysing the books in the European Picture Book Collection

T his chapter applies the semiotic text analysis framework (STA) set out in the last chapter to the theme of 'friendship' in the EPBC. Each category of the framework is discussed, focusing on the people, setting and story in the narratives. The chapter concludes with an evaluation of the analysis, and suggests the implications for using such a collection to facilitate a European dimension in primary education.

Although all the EPBC books have the potential for being analysed under any of the three classifications of people, setting and story, each has been assigned to that which facilitates the most detailed analysis. The semiotic text analysis framework (See Table 3, p.51) is applied with references to each book's individual strengths of visual communication. Relevant connections are made with *Category 1: visual codes*, which feeds into and overlaps with *Category 2: visual narrative techniques*. The books are then considered against *Category 3: types of picture book* and *Category 4: picture book ingredients*, in terms of how much the visual representations contribute to universal understandings of these picture book narratives.

Theme

The most powerful universal theme of this EPBC is 'friendship', which presents itself on a number of different levels in each book. The books are analysed under three sub-themes: friendship in the dark; friendship and responsibility; friendship and relationships, and these are considered under the three picture book Classifications: People; Setting; Story. The overall theme of 'friendship' in each picture book is treated quite distinctly, as each country approaches the concept from a slightly different angle and uses its own range of visual codes and narrative techniques.

Classification: People
Sub-theme: friendship in the dark

The analysis is first applied to: the visual development of the people in the stories and the thematic link between them. Each book had originally been chosen for its intensive visual focus on the development of characterisation within the narratives. How illustrators use facial expressions and bodily stance, for example, is crucial to the development of the protagonists in the books from Finland, France, Italy and Belgium, all of whom have different, yet recognisable attitudes to finding friendship in the dark while experiencing fear, confidence, reluctance, dominance and enjoyment.

VEM *ska trösta knyttet? (Who will comfort Toffle?)* Finland

Category 1 – Visual codes: The diminutive figure of Toffle is introduced on the first page (fig.3). This sorrowful creature is presented cowering, a colourless pen and ink child, looking out of his enclosed frame with wide eyes, expressing his fear of the dark, visually communicated through his clutching of a small lamp. Positioned in the lower-right half of the frame, in a subservient position, he is alone and seemingly helpless. The only colour in this setting is the yellow of the light bulbs which Toffle appears to be lighting to comfort himself and perhaps allay his terror. The sombreness of this lonely character is positioned in strong contrast with the blues, greens and blacks on the opposite page, where bats and other apparently menacing night creatures prowl around outside Toffle's home in an almost surreal way.

The mottled effect of this small character and his home is contrasted with the crisp and definite colours of the night creatures who, although they are obviously frightening to Toffle, have a slight air of fun about them. They are carrying umbrellas, portrayed in a dominating position at the top of the page, which has no frame to restrict their power. The reader is invited to empathise with Toffle, yet given visual encouragement to see that the night might not be as menacing as it first appears.

Category 2 – Visual narrative techniques: Throughout the book, the essence of narrative is shown by the emotion engendered in Toffle's characterisation. He is looked down upon as an insignificant figure, who almost disappears into the background as he tries to escape from his frightening world. The uncertainty of his existence is depicted in the broken brush and pen strokes of Tove Jansson, while reality is conveyed to readers in clear definite colours. As daylight comes, brighter sweeps of colour, patterning and circumstantial details adorn the peripheral characters of the story, but Toffle remains grey. The turning point comes when the protagonist realises that he is not the only one in need of comfort. His night-time uncertainty, shown in broken black and white strokes, becomes solid colour. He can now frighten the awful 'groke' because he wants to comfort a new-found friend. His profile and determined expression, together with the movement of his little arms and legs, are trigger images which allow the reader to predict what is likely to happen and be prepared for the story's denouement.

67

Figure 3: in *VEM ska trösta knyttet?* (Jansson, 1984: 1)
A diminutive figure who is frightened of the dark.

Category 3 – Types of picture book: In *VEM ska trösta knyttet?* much of the story is related by pages of almost completely black and white images alternating with brightly coloured pages. The former portray the darkness of Toffle's world, the latter the bright life of those around him. It is up to the reader to make the link between the two sets of images and follow the frightened creature when he eventually joins the colourful world of friendship. Any reading of this text would make use of its 'indeterminate' features, jumping from one scene to another without too much explanation.

Category 4 – Picture book ingredients: The ingredients of this picture book contribute to an understanding of how texts can work on a number of levels. The universal theme is one of being lonely but finding out, in this secondary world, that there is often someone who feels even lonelier than you. The concept of childhood is expressed through semiotic characterisation and fantasy relationships which draw on personal intertextual experiences, making this text an extremely powerful communicative tool. Although not a specifically Finnish book, the darkness of the country for so many months of the year comes through in the illustrations.

Une nuit, un chat... (One night, a cat...) France

Category 1 – Visual codes: This protagonist has an air of self assurance and well-being, circularly framed (fig.4). He, too, is going out at night and is concerned about his first 'sortie' but the definite colours and shapes of Yvan Pommaux's illustrations suggest that Groucho is a cat with confidence, albeit with a little apprehension beneath veneer. His parents are there to support him on his first night of adventure – hence his bravado. While his anxious parents watch, against the backdrop of Parisian rooftops, the hero ventures forth out of the right side of the frame, leading the reader towards his first adventure. Blues, blacks and greens again dominate the night-time scene, but the menace is in the observer's mind: what will become of the kitten? But his father is ever ready to protect him, walking in the shadows along the rooftops, prepared to pounce on whatever enemy might be lurking in the darkness. These pages are in sharp contrast to those containing the lively youngster depicted in carefree activities and unhindered by the constricting frames of the pictures which contain his parents.

Category 2 – Visual narrative techniques: Groucho is going out at night for the first time, and his story is totally on the horizontal plane, possibly indicating the normality of his existence. He is leaving a very caring environment, emphasised by earlier circumstantial details of his treasured belongings such as a toy car strategically placed on his bedroom floor. But when the sewer rat appears in the darkness the calmness of the scene fragments. Domination is assured by Rat's surprise appearance from the bottom right-hand side of the

Figure 4: in *Une nuit, un chat...* (Pommaux, 1994: 27)
A cat with confidence!

69

double page spread and the zigzag bubble in which his name is printed, intimating anger and discord. Red is added to the colours, hinting at potential conflict and possible bloodshed. The ensuing pages continue to engender emotion cinematically, showing the speed of movement across a two page spread. Finally, a mere centimetre of tail shows that the light-hearted and carefree Groucho has returned home unharmed. The slight upward stroke depicting his mouth on the next page, smiles as he announces his wish to go out again the next night. A wish that is cosily framed in a circle of parental care and concern, not dissimilar from the protecting oval shell shape which engulfs Toffle in his new-found security.

Category 3 – Types of picture book: Through fantasy, this tale plays on the ability of the picture book to exaggerate situations while still retaining a certain credibility. The larger than life sewer rat who provides the conflict in the story could be seen as an element of excess, going beyond the bounds of realism as he leaps off the page. Alongside the more conformist felines, he is expressed in extravagant imagery.

Category 4 – Picture book ingredients: A caring relationship between parents and children permeates this visual text, creating a fantasy character set within a real situation with which children universally can empathise. Drawing on personal childhood experiences, the narrative explores picture book ingredients which create opportunities for discussion and development. The theme is not particularly French, yet the visuals, specifically the Parisian rooftops and the 'chic-ness' of Groucho's night-time friends, provide a stimulus for intercultural exploration.

La bambina che non voleva andare a dormire
(The little girl who didn't want to go to bed) Italy

Category 1 – Visual codes: Here, too, we find a determined character not unlike Groucho. Pinin Carpi shows Anna striding across the front page of this text, full of confidence. Like many young children, she is reluctant to go to bed and does everything she can think of to delay the moment when she will be alone in the darkness. Colour is used only on the front cover. Yet the black and white line drawings depict this child in both real and fantasy worlds, where putting the colour is in the mind of the readers as their eyes are drawn into each scene.

Category 2 – Visual narrative techniques: In Anna's bedtime stories she is always in a position of power (fig.5), in much the same way as she is with her long-suffering father who is telling the stories. Over time, she is seen on a motor bike racing against her father who is on a camel; wielding a sword as he is defeated in battle; or knighting him as one of her many subjects. The joy of these stories is in the intricate circumstantial details that are woven into a narrative simplicity, enabling each reader to bring personal experiences to the text.

Category 3 – Types of picture book: Opportunities are created for 'boundary breaking' to occur within the narrative. The bedtime tales are recounted as Anna tells them but space is provided for readers to write their own invented story, too. So the book can be read and re-read with a personal contribution from the young readers each time, who become part of the story itself.

Category 4 – Picture book ingredients: In the minutely detailed portrayals of Anna's many bedtime tales, in which she is always the star, universal intertextual, iconic links such as *Little Red Riding Hood* and *Mickey Mouse* abound. Empathy with Anna is assured through the variety of semiotic picture book ingredients involved in this story. Reality is interwoven with private childhood fantasies, creating a variety of possible worlds to be shared by others. The Italian songs with which the book ends (recorded onto cassette) facilitate some cultural awareness of the music and language of Italian children.

70

Figure 5: in *La bambina che non voleva andare a dormire*
(Carpi, 1996: 10/14/16) – Anna, in a position of power.

Un jour mon Prince viendra (One day my Prince will come) Belgium

Category 1 – Visual codes: Power is what Marguerite also appears to have as she gallops across the fields in search of her prince. Framed within the orange hues of a setting sun against the sparse countryside, fine lines express her discontentment. Only the small frog in her cloak and her spindly hands that clasp the horns of a ram tell readers that this is no ordinary person. Marguerite is a witch and her character unfolds through the somewhat menacing darkness of the illustrations. Her water-colour unreal world inhabited by frogs and toads surrounds her, as she makes her way home through the darkness to her solitary house.

Category 2 – Visual narrative techniques: Marguerite is lonely and, like Toffle, longs for a companion. Andréa Nève's fine line drawings, often in a perspective that looks up at this domineering character (reminiscent of Keeping's work) show her brown-hazed despair. Loneliness is everywhere, heightened by a mass of circumstantial details like the spider's web in her hair which denotes the passage of time as she waits. Power is all that Marguerite knows. Her only way of communicating is to hurl unspeakable demands at prospective suitors. This she does to an unsuspecting snowman believing him to be her prince. Marguerite is visually elevated to the central position on the page through 'movement' lines which push her up into the most dominant position possible. From here her spindly hand and pointed fingers can focus her demands, reinforced by the darkness of her semi-opened mouth and a forehead line signifying anger, while her hair is propelled upwards with minute black lines almost like fire-crackers. Her hand on her hip completes the image of control, the picture emotively conveys an essence of narrative unrestricted by frame.

Category 3 – Types of picture book: This is an amusing book because it makes fun of the conventional. It is a *parody* of normal tradition; usually it is the beautiful princess who finally finds her handsome prince. Parody expresses a refusal to accept a situation which is culturally determined (Lewis, 1994); in *Un jour mon Prince viendra*, the European fairytale heritage is being turned upside-down by a belligerent witch – who finally ensnares the rather ordinary village baker.

Category 4 – Picture book ingredients: At the story's conclusion Marguerite realises that she doesn't have to bully or dominate in order to find friendship – a universal theme which touches the lives of many children throughout Europe. The picture book ingredients which contribute to this parodic narrative encompass many of the attributes assigned to Category 4. The fantasy secondary world of this picture book provides a backdrop for the characterisation of the protagonist which relies heavily on semiotic representations, intertextuality and the metafictive to create such powerful images.

Figure 6: in *Un jour mon Prince viendra* (Nève and Crowther, 1995: 20)
Marguerite hurls demands at her 'prince'.

Lotje is jarig (Lotje's birthday) **Belgium**

Category 1 – Visual codes: Witches have always been a popular ingredient of Belgian children's books says Annemie Leyson (in Cotton, 1996). She chose Lieve Baeten's book because she felt that the character of Lotje is set within a world full of magic which reflects the cosiness of Flemish homes. Lotje is a cheerful apprentice witch who has no fears of the dark, nor does she wish to dominate. It is her birthday and she wants to have fun, suggested by the bright, cheerful colours against the background of the night sky – a sky which is full of lightness provided by the moon and a star hanging outside her tree-house. She is looking forward to the celebrations, as indicated by the pert little smile on her face. She is also keen to conjure up a cake for her birthday but when she cannot, she simply enjoys the dark.

Category 2 – Visual narrative techniques: A sequence of images suggest Lotje's antics (fig.7). Night is portrayed as a time of enjoyment and excitement; gone are the menacing, harsh blues and greens of Toffle's world. Here light pastel shades are enhanced with the warm yellows, reds and oranges of the child herself. Even the door sheds light through its smiling face, a trigger image which activates a positive response to the whole narrative. Later the emotion engendered in this narrative is portrayed through shades of colouring, and this becomes more poignant when the dejected figure of Lotje is shown in a blue night with no light relief. Losing her cat makes her sad but help is near in the shape of protective aunts who swish through the sky above, allowing perceptive readers to realise that rescue is imminent. Finally Lotje makes her spells work, as a series of circumstantial details show, and she conjures up her lost cat.

Category 3 – Types of picture book: This Belgian book is also a 'parody' – a parody of birthdays. Conventionally, children invite magicians to their parties as entertainment, but what if the birthday child herself is the entertainment? Lotje lives in a world of magic and excitement and all she wants for her birthday is to have a cake and be with her cat. Eventually both become possible ... only because she knows the words 'Hocus Pocus Pompelmoes', which have their equivalents in most European languages.

Category 4 – Picture book ingredients: The carefree world of darkness, light and excitement contrasts with the dominance of Marguerite in the book from the French speaking part of Belgium. Witches are the theme of both Belgian books, and so is the importance of friendship and belonging. The colours used in *Lotje is jarig* suggest a warmth in the relationship of the characters as well as the primary meaning of the pleasure of having a birthday. This specific connotation depicting close family ties and celebrations is part of the ideology of many European cultures. It should be discussed with children as an important visual ingredient of characterisation in picture books.

Figure 7: in *Lotje is jarig* (Baeten, 1996: 2)
A carefree world of darkness, light and excitement.

Classification: Setting
Sub-theme: friendship and responsibility

The thematic analysis in this section is applied to books which present culturally different settings yet relate to a similar universal theme: children in roles of responsibility. The EPBC books from Sweden, Scotland, Spain, Denmark, Ireland and Wales all place their characters visually within cultural contexts that are interpreted by their creators. Although all the stories have their own distinctive settings, some of them make visual cultural references which go beyond the world that all children inhabit.

Kan du vissla Johanna (Can you whistle Johanna?) Sweden

Category 1 – Visual codes: Ulf Stark and Anna Höglund's book allows its characters to inhabit not only the world of children but also that of old people. Two boys, Beera and Jag, are outside a brightly coloured 'Konditori' (cake-shop), signifying the 'alive' world of the children. This is contrasted with a grey footpath alongside the cake-shop which leads from the bottom of the verso page and meanders towards the top of the recto; passing on its way a grey church, a line of black hearses and a grey-brown nursing home (fig.8). Here live the old people, from among whom Beera will adopt a grandfather; an old man who appears to be, in the words of Marie Louise Olofson who chose the book, almost 'on a conveyor belt to death'. Even the birds are absent from the trees on the recto page, as are all signs of life.

Once inside the old people's home, lines of institutionalisation come into play. Readers are taken from the open outside world into the framed, circular existence of the old. The regular lines of perspective draw the eye towards a nothingness at the end of a long corridor; all the doors are the same, save for the first, which the two boys are about to enter. One gets the impression that Grandpa will work his way along the corridor to his own nothingness or death. The lightness from the other side of his door, however, affords a little hope in the life of this old man, and for the children.

Category 2 – Visual narrative techniques: Everything in the nursing home is represented in two-dimensional, regular shapes and institutionalised lines, within which the old people conform and are distanced from reality. It is only when the children take Grandpa outside that the rigid framework disappears and the environment takes shape. As they leave the home circumstantial details of a square tiled floor and formidable, hands-on- hips, uniformed nurse are replaced by a winding path, green trees and birds signifying life. Emotion is engendered in the narrative as life continues with the antics of the three 'children'. Even though darkness is falling, Grandpa still manages to climb trees, scrump cherries and sit on the floor eating round doughnuts, surrounded by the countryside, trees and stars. He smokes a cigar and blows

Figure 8: in *Kan du vissla Johanna* (Stark and Höglund, 1992: 6/7)
The conveyor belt to death?

smoke rings, a circular icon of his contentment, before being returned to the blackness of the path that leads 'home'.

Category 3 – Types of picture book: Visually, this picture book is presented rather like a film strip. It rarely uses cinematic conventions, yet the detailed images follow each other in such a way that the environment inhabited by the children and Grandpa evolves with every turn of the page. There is almost an 'excess' of visuals to give information about the setting of this story. It could be said to be 'over the top' (Lewis, 1994: 30) in terms of detail, as the culturally specific, explicit visual references to the nursing home and funeral scenes may not be universally understood. Within the context of the narrative, however, this extravagant imagery highlights the poignancy and the importance of the relationship between the children and Grandpa.

Category 4 – Picture book ingredients: *Kan du vissla Johanna* deals with everyday life situations in Sweden concerning human relationships. Insights are given into children's unconventional ways of thinking and problem solving and into how Swedish society treats old people. In spite of the rather bleak picture painted of old age in Sweden, this is a humorous book, telling a universal story which shows how much fun you can have with a grandfather or a grandson. It contains many picture book ingredients and depicts relationships between the generations in a light-hearted way, yet the fundamental social situation is never underplayed. It is the little things that are so important, like taking a flower or a cigar to your grandfather or having him teach you to whistle. The underlying theme is of friendship and its importance between generations.

Katie Morag and the new pier – Scotland

Category 1 – Visual codes: This also focuses on the relationship between the old and young. Katie Morag's (real) grandmother fears the changes happening in her life. In contrast with the Swedish book, Mairi Hedderwick's illustrations are full of optimism in their details and in the lightness of colour. Alan Hill (in Cotton, 1996) suggests that one of the outstanding features of this book is the vivid life conveyed by the minutia of information in the pictures; no matter how many times one reads it one can always find something new in their many circumstantial details. The front-page of the book sets the scene with a lightness of brush strokes, grey-green hues and gentle perspective, conveying the atmosphere of a sleepy fishing village. Centre stage are Katie Morag, her grandmother and her dog, all looking rather glum. As Katie Morag puts a reassuring hand on her grandmother's knee, it is clear that it will be the child who plays a comforting role in this story.

78

Category 2 – Visual narrative techniques: The new pier is Grannie Island's worry, and the divided loyalties between the old and the new are portrayed visually throughout the book. None are better placed than in the village store, where the central page divides grandmother and granddaughter (fig.9). Katie Morag on the left, hands together, looks expectantly as the villagers discuss their future, while Grannie Island on the right looks sceptical, her arms folded in resignation. Even the dog appears to mirror her feelings – a trigger image which activates a response to the whole narrative. The busy islanders seem oblivious of this central vignette. Hedderwick pays great attention to circumstantial detail in this scene: everything is labelled; a young child shows his drawing to the postmistress; workers show their politeness and integration within the community; a baby plays in its cradle; a dog is sneakily fed a biscuit while nobody is looking; and conversations are generally shared. The epitome of Scottish rural village life is depicted in these expressive visuals.

Figure 9: in *Katie Morag and the new pier* (Hedderwick, 1993: 4/5)
Attention to detail: The old and the new.

79

Category 3 – Types of picture book: The initial sequence of visuals in *Katie Morag and the new pier* alternates between outdoor and indoor vignettes of life on the fictitious Scottish island of Struay and readers are invited to make links between the images in order to build up an understanding of both setting and situation. This picture book could be classified under 'indeterminacy' for, even though the pictures unfold rather like a film script, readers still have to make connections between these events in order to create a narrative.

Category 4 – Picture book ingredients: At the point in the story where the pier is threatened, Hedderwick uses the double page spread to the full and allows the sea waves to swish and swirl across the pages. The tempestuous blues and greens practically envelope the small red ferryboat, steered by Granny Island who has realised that she can be part of the change. Finally, when a variety of picture book ingredients have been exhibited, darkness calmly and serenely descends over the sleeping village. The new pier is in place and the greyness of night has a somewhat optimistic hue; the warmth of the yellows from the moon, the pier and one or two small houses suggest harmony between old and new. In fact the scene is so convincing that travel agents keep getting requests for tickets to Struay from adults who want to share the island's tranquility!

El guardián del olvido (The guardian of lost things) Spain

Category 1 – Visual codes: The scene is set for Juan Manuel Gisbert and Alfonso Ruano's visually Spanish tale through a series of cinematic devices. A big close up of two small hands holding a spinning top give the focus for the story. A mid-close-up of the boy, Gabriel, then appears, followed by a larger mid-shot of the enigmatic Analisa framed by a window from which she is gazing. A long shot establishes the school playground, followed by a close-up of eyes – Analisa's – watching, as Gabriel realises that his spinning top is missing. The ensuing long-shot shows both the journey of the two children to find the guardian of lost things, and their arrival at his mysterious house. The flatness of walls and regimented windows reflect the browness of the Spanish landscape and when Gabriel is invited to find his lost toy in a room full of lost things, shuttered windows keep out the light. Later, as he searches for his mother's lost watch, the room is full of visual references to Spanish artists.

Category 2 – Visual narrative techniques: The surreal, timeless setting of this book is achieved not only through cinematic techniques and trigger images such as the spinning top, but also in the way the illustrator uses light and shade. In the room of time, where Gabriel encounters the work of artists such as Salvador Dali, he and the guardian are bathed in white light, framed in the doorway (fig.10), almost as if a spell has been cast. Escape is practically

Figure 10: in *El guardián del olvido* (Gisbert and Ruano, 1990: 18/19)
Visual references to Spanish artist Dali.

impossible from this distant, unreal world filled with iconic images and circumstantial detail. This is where Gabriel finally manages to find Analisa after a long search – a lost object now found by a new friend.

Category 3 – Types of picture book: El guardián del olvido has a tendency towards 'excess'; its surreal imagery could be described as 'over the top' (Lewis, 1994: 30), going beyond the realms of realism. Gabriel is taken by Analisa from his secure school environment into an unbelievable world in which all the lost things imaginable have been collected; their representations are a feast for the eyes and facilitate much intertextual activity.

Category 4 – Picture book ingredients: The smoothness of colour and line in this book create an unreal world, slightly tinged with mystery and fear. Gabriel does not really understand Analisa and nor do the readers, yet the ingredients of this picture book amalgamate to create a haunting story with a friendship theme that can be universally understood. Cultural references to Spain's arid, brown environment and to its artistic heritage enrich the illustrations and are a marked contrast with the settings for the Swedish and Scottish books.

Mosekonens Bryg (The marsh people) Denmark

Category 1 – Visual codes: Ib Spang Olsen's Danish folktale is also told through unique style and imagery – the entire story is depicted in varied shades of green, presenting an overwhelming sense of growth and fertility. The story is set in a characteristic Danish landscape, notes Mogens Jansen (in Cotton, 1996b), explaining that the fog is steaming above the marsh because the marsh people are boiling water for their beer. These folkloric characters sleep deep down in the earth and the children emerge only to help their parents with preparations for creating the Spring. The unusual illustrations produce a certain magical mystery around this event but, unlike the austere and distant guardian in the Spanish book, the marsh children are not just down to earth but also of the earth.

Category 2 – Visual narrative techniques: These children are depicted in earth colours, earth textures, and appear almost part of the earth (fig.11). Their actions unfold through mid to long shots, allowing little intimacy with individuals. The cartoon-like series of interactions with other earthly creatures, triggered by a variety of circumstantial details, creates a collective view of the busy Marsh people, rather than focusing on specific characters. This folkloric community is drawn into the light when the sun reaches its height in the sky. Toiling can then cease and warmth be enjoyed in a setting where practically all traces of green have disappeared and a pinky haze sets above the marsh. The Danish Spring has arrived.

Figure 11: in *Mosekonens Bryg* (Olsen, 1994: 26/27)
A sense of growth and fertility.

Category 3 – Types of Picture Book: This book is difficult to classify. In many cultures it could be said to be a 'parody' of the arrival of Spring, as it almost makes fun of conventional beliefs. But for Danish people it is part of their heritage and, as such, needs considered explanation and discussion.

Category 4: Picture book ingredients: Although there are many picture book ingredients, this is probably the most difficult EPBC book in which to comprehend a universal childhood theme. The fantasy setting, semiotically represented, reflects at one level the secondary world ideology of a culture of helping parents, which is easily recognisable. The concept of brewing beer to facilitate the Spring is less easy to understand, although thought-provoking in terms of cultural comparisons.

Naomh Pádraig agus Crom Dubh (St Patrick and Crom Dubh) Ireland

Category 1 – Visual codes: Shades of green, not surprisingly, feature in this book but the story of a medieval pagan being converted to Christianity, aided and abetted by his young servant, is predominantly illustrated in vivid colours. Yellows, particularly around the haloed head of St. Patrick, reflect the godliness of the subject (fig.12). St Patrick is trying to convey to Crom Dubh, through his young messenger, the importance of God. He does this by rejecting three large hams he is offered and replacing them with the written words 'Deo Gratias' which he gives to the young boy. As Crom Dubh is unhappy with this exchange he is forced to visit the saint himself, only to be shown that 'Deo Gratias' written three times in black and white carries more weight than three large, brightly coloured hams.

Figure 12: in *Naomh Pádraig agus Crom Dubh* (Rosenstock, 1995: 26/7) 'Deo Gratias' carries more weight.

Category 2 – Visual narrative techniques: In this final scene, the upward sweeps of yellow move the three lines of 'Deo Gratias' into an almost heavenly position, driven by the intimate close-up of St Patrick. In contrast, the three hams are pulled downwards away from the less important mid-shot character – denoting the opposing directions of both the concrete objects and the thinking of St Patrick and Crom Dubh. The cartoon style Christian and pagan iconic images are set against a background of heavenly blues and pinks with a dove flying from Crom Dubh towards St Patrick, symbolising the pagan's conversion to Christianity, in a world replete with circumstantial details.

Category 3 – Types of picture book: Although the cartoon format suggests an 'indeterminacy' which is built upon absence of information, the servant boy's initial journey to and from Crom Dubh is sequential. It is only when the second and third journeys with the hams are undertaken that readers have to fill in the gaps to facilitate comprehension.

Category 4 – Picture book ingredients: Confrontation and misunderstanding occur in most children's lives. This universal childhood theme, set in a secondary fantasy world, reflects in its characterisation and relationships an ideology which permeates many Catholic countries, yet relates to all cultures. So the ways in which St Patrick avoids conflict are particularly pertinent and these are conveyed through a number of picture book ingredients which allow individual interpretations of the folktale.

Cantre'r Gwaelod (Cities in the sea) Wales

Category 1 – Visual codes: Siân Lewis and Jackie Morris's Welsh folktale also addresses a universal theme: that 'Pride comes before a fall'. It has been chosen because this well-loved Welsh story is reflected in other cultures, especially the Celtic imagery which echoes the *Cathédrale Engloutie* (submerged cathedral), a Breton myth from the North West of France.

The watery landscapes of blues and greens are pictured in a medieval folkloric style, where the position of the characters defines the opening and closing of the tale. A royal father shows his son the lands that will one day be his: idyllic lands across a double spread give the impression that the inheritance is endless, the minute, finely detailed royal subjects working in harmony with this unspoiled vista. The downfall of the king and his people is due to an excess of imbibing; food and drink are portrayed in a number of active images as the community prepares for a night of feasting. The excitement and activity move across the pages as wild boar, sweetmeats and other fare are carried towards the banqueting hall. A mass of browns, reds and muted blues not only express the seriousness of the eating but dwell also in detail on the food that is to be consumed.

85

Category 2 – Visual narrative techniques: Unfortunately, the king and his subjects are so involved in the detailed festivities that they do not heed the warning from the young boy, who urges his father to close the city flood gates. Disharmony is reinforced by the positioning of the child on one side of a double page spread and the King opposite, facing him, thus evoking confrontation (fig.13). Dominance is uncertain: although the boy is on the left, the height of the heads remains equal. The lack of interest shown by the king and his insistence on continuing the celebrations are trigger images for signalling the disaster which is to befall the city. As the revellery continues, the sea, unimpeded by man-made barriers, engulfs the city. The final iconic image is that of the father and son looking out to sea from right to left, looking back and visually closing the story with a sea-blue calm nothingness to replace the fertile, opening landscapes of their earlier realm. The initial and final imagery resonates with the cinematic technique used by John Ford in his film *The Searchers* (1956), where the opening and closing of doors signifies the beginning and end of his story.

Category 3 – Types of picture book: 'Indeterminacy' is the tentative category for a picture book whose cinematic tale jumps from one scene to another. The reader is invited to complete the narrative and become absorbed in the culturally representative visuals depicting this Celtic tale.

86 *Category 4 – Picture book ingredients*: Immersion into a secondary, fantasy world of legendary folktale, through the ingredients of this picture book, creates a sense of what Bettleheim (1976:5) suggests will stimulate imagination, help to develop intellect and clarify emotions. The story creates empathy with both father and son, trying to develop an understanding of the actions of both. It is a universal theme which has no cultural preference.

Figure 13: in *Cantre'r Gwaelod* (Lewis and Morris, 1996: 20/21)
Pride comes before a fall.

Classification: Story
Sub-theme: friendship and relationships

Illustrative sequences which give readers work to do contribute to a greater understanding of narrative structure, especially for 8-11 year olds. This section analyses the books from the Netherlands, Northern Ireland, Greece, Germany, Luxembourg, Austria, Portugal and England, which all do this. Their universal theme, as with the previous books, is the concept of relationships with friends and between nations.

Kees en Keetje (Kees and Keetje) The Netherlands

Category 1 – Visual codes: Here is a picture sequence which wholly depends upon the readers' ability to see relationships between objects and to draw inferences. The pen and ink drawings by Jantien Buisman tell an uncluttered tale of a friendship which becomes stale, breaks up and comes together again because of the specific needs of both parties. Although the book contains thirty detailed sketches, the beginning, middle and end (the bare bones of the story) can be highlighted in just three of the pictures (fig.14). The visual narrative begins with two friends (the female hedgehog wearing a small brightly coloured headscarf which contrasts with the black and white of the remainder of the scene) going about their household duties together. Anything is possible.

Category 2 – Visual narrative techniques: As the story progresses, the storyline becomes more probable and the narrative develops through a sequence of images. It is apparent that the friends are not in accord when they are seen rejecting each others' company in a number of situations, including the archetypal avoidance strategy of sitting back to back at the breakfast table. Circumstantial details are the focus for this visual, displaying traditional Dutch breakfast fare. One can only speculate about what is being said, but the effect on both characters can be determined because both are visible; showing only one of them would have been insufficient to create the mood. Not only do they have their backs to each other but a large expanse of page lies between them, emphasising the enormity of the rift.

On the ensuing pages the two characters continue avoiding one another until, one day, they pass each other, Kees carrying a conical bag of chips and Keetje a jar of apple sauce. Both realise at once that they cannot eat their favourite Dutch meal of chips and apple sauce unless they get together! So the story ends with their making up. This simple visual narrative engenders emotion and encompasses the tensions and tribulations of relationships.

Category 3 – Types of picture book: All stories are built upon absence, suggests Lewis (1994:32). Readers are not given all the information so the stories could theoretically be assigned to the category of 'indeterminacy' (see

87

Figure 14: in *Kees En Keetje* (Buisman, 1976: 3/15/45)
A simple visual narrative structure.

Chapter Six). This would appear to be the case for *Kees en Keetje*. Although the picture sequencing is clear, the visuals jump from one room in the house to another so rapidly that the reader has to fill in the gaps and compensate for the lack of explicit cohesion.

Category 4 – Picture book ingredients: Careful attention is paid to fine details of character and plot. Through facial expressions, body movements and the visual progression of the storyline, this picture book's ingredients have the potential to contribute to readers' growing command and understanding of narrative.

War and Peas – **Northern Ireland**

Category 1 – Visual codes: Portraying vivid characterisation by means of colour, size and movement, Michael Foreman's cartoon-like parody achieves a clarity of narrative through visuals showing a poor country seeking aid from a rich neighbour. In the opening 'shots', King Lion is shown as a washed-out character, facing his subjects with a resigned air about the plight of his country. His slightly lowered outstretched arms suggest the weight of the world on his shoulders and he does not know what to do to help his subjects. Both he and his people are so lightly drawn that they almost fade into insignificance on the white page. It is difficult to know what he could do to save them from starvation.

89

Category 2 – Visual narrative techniques: The emotion is evoked by from the visuals which cause readers to empathise with King Lion who, portrayed from a high level viewpoint, appears weak and insignificant. Obviously he will need to seek help from a rich, colourful, prestigious and well-fed, neighbour – Fat King. The lion's journey through mountainous lands, across pages filled with circumstantial details of gluttony and food, paves the way for a first encounter with the overpowering monarch. Large and centre-left of the verso page, Fat King dominates a double spread, his robes flowing onto the recto where, almost unnoticed and blending in with the background, appears the quaking lion.

King Lion has come seeking help, but the probable outcome indicated in this portrayal of the scene is that the cartoon-like Fat King and his armed army guards will give no help. This turns out to be the case. But in the ensuing battle of green peas, cakes and jellies, Fat King and his fat army are hoist with their own petard, leaving King Lion and his country to benefit from the spoils of war. In the final frame King Lion, in stronger colours, is seen victorious. He cycles home to his waiting people, a semi-circular rainbow of hope positioned towards the top right-hand side of the picture. Whereas Fat King, now coloured in blacks and purples, sinks lower and lower out of the illustration, possibly towards death.

Figure 15: in *War and Peas* (Foreman, 1978: 10/11)
Mountainous lands of food tower above King Lion.

Category 3 – Types of picture book: Given its over-the-top quality in terms of the over-sized king, his army and his food, one might be tempted to classify this book in terms of 'excess'. But 'parody' is even more accurate, as the serious nature of the continuing friction between England and Northern Ireland is depicted as an allegory.

Category 4 – Picture book ingredients: Fat King's actions unintentionally provide his neighbours with a means of helping themselves and this book was chosen because it provides a way for complex or difficult ideas about the relationship of nation states and different peoples to be communicated to young children (Marriott in Cotton, 1996). Dealing with these concepts in an allegorical fashion, using a number of picture book ingredients, is made even more accessible by illustrations that use colour wash, line and page layout to suggest mood, honour and drama.

The story-spinner meets the sugar-wizard – Greece

Category 1 – Visual codes: Food is again central to this story, set in a young child's fantasy world. The pen and ink story-spinner distances himself from his home surroundings to explore the world of 'caramelos' – the sweets that can be seen in his thoughts. He flies up out of the picture on his journey, leaving behind a sugar house with oval-shaped smoke coming from the roof – an image familiar in childhood drawings in many European cultures. The winding path and rounded shape of the single tree are also typical. Anything is possible in this imaginary world inhabited by the story-spinner. Although he is adult, as shown by his moustache, glasses and white hair, he lives in the world of childhood – a suitable habitat for a teller of stories.

Category 2 – Visual narrative techniques: The sweets that are constantly on the story-spinner's mind are a thread running throughout the book and they provide the emotional pull which is the essence of this narrative. The idea of longing for sweets and other sugary things (which can be provided by the sugar-wizard from another country) permeates the story and guides readers through a number of adventures, highlighted with specific circumstantial details. The two protagonists, story-spinner and sugar-wizard, tour the sweet-making factory in a sequence of images conveying the passage of time. They are shown as diminutive black and white figures, in contrast with the larger-than-life makers of 'manna from heaven' (fig.16). This central sequence is portrayed in a montage of shots, also using child-like images, which depict the stages of making the sweets. On the first floor, shown by ink zig-zags, there is a hint that all is not quite as idyllic as it first appeared. Two chefs, one looking happier than the other, begin the confectionery process. The cooking of these delicacies is shown more centrally on the page, with the finished product below.

Figure 16: in *The story-spinner meets the sugar-wizard* (Kyritsopoulus, 1985: 30/31)
Larger than life factory workers.

As the story develops, the story-spinner becomes more relaxed in the cordial company of his host, the sugar-wizard, and his caramelos. But he eats too many sweets and begins to feel sick and he longs to be at home, eating normally again.

Category 3 – Types of picture book: Although set within a fantasy world, this text explores the real concept of greed and longing. The layout of the book lends itself to 'indeterminacy' as each page sees the story-spinner setting out on another adventure, leaving the reader to fill in the gaps.

Category 4 – Picture book ingredients: 'Having too much of a good thing' is a universal theme by no means unique to Greece, and including the book in the EPBC affords opportunities for comparison of such cultural similarity. By its use of many picture book ingredients and its focus on linguistic differences the visual narrative structure is enhanced.

Hallo, kleiner Wal (Hello, little whale) **Germany**

Category 1 – Visual codes: This picture book tells a more complex tale, which is made visually accessible through its vivid colouring and clarity of images. An old couple inhabit a north German village near the sea, where it often snows. Their quiet life is enlivened by the visit from a young whale twice a year – but then the visits stop. The villagers try to help by building a snow-whale but nothing can cheer the elderly pair. After about eighteen months they put a little boat on their sledge and set off across the frozen landscape in search of their friend. The poignancy of their journey and the enormity of the quest is indicated by the smallness of their mode of transport and the vastness of first the frozen white landscape and, later, the deep blue sea.

Category 2 – Visual narrative techniques: The essence of this narrative is encapsulated in four cartoon-format images conveying the passage of time, during which the friends are re-united (fig.17). When the couple eventually reach the sea, they fall asleep, so fail to see the predictive detail which the illustrator provides: water spouting out above the ocean's surface, suggesting that a whale might be close by. When they wake up, the dark blue of the sea which has carried the couple is suddenly replaced by what appears to be a large rock. Closer inspection of the rock, as it rises slightly in the sea, reveals an eye. The fourth picture shows that the couple have actually landed on top of their old friend – who has grown rather bigger!

The visual sequencing, combined with trigger images relating to the whale, are vital to an understanding of this and subsequent sequential patterning. These images contrasting the smallness of the elderly people with the large greyness of the whale continue when a female whale appears with their small offspring. The final iconographic image shows the two large mammals swim-

93

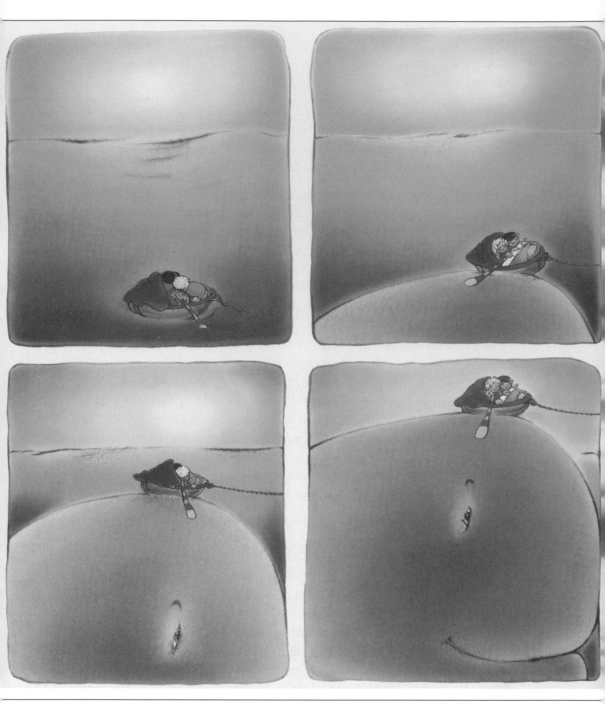

Figure 17: in *Hallo, kleiner Wal* (Kalow and Bröger, 1996: 17)
A narrative encapsulated in four images.

ming alongside each other, with two minute shapes in-between ... one red, the old people's boat, and one grey. The couple have found the small whale.

Category 3 – Types of picture book: The cinematic conventions used in this book, which jump from one scene to another as the elderly couple prepare for and undertake their journey, would seem to place this text within the category of 'indeterminacy'. Although the visual narrative at first appears quite clear, there are many circumstantial details that require readers to keep re-reading the images to make sure that a complete, personal interpretation of the story has been gained.

Category 4 – Picture book ingredients: The picture book ingredients of this semiotic fantasy world create a narrative which focuses on friendship and trust between humans and animals. The integral underlying relationships are universal and, set within an unusual Germanic setting, provide an entrée into aspects of European life which may be unknown to a good many young readers.

D'Grisette an D'Choupette um motorrad
(Grisette and Choupette on a motor cycle) Luxembourg

Category 1 – Visual codes: Anne-Marie Theis and Mariette Ries's picture book is written in three languages: Luxembourgish, French and German. Two young mice are sprawled lazily across the first page, not knowing what to do with themselves. They appear to be on holiday and at a loose end. Half-eaten, oversized fruit and vegetables are scattered across the floor, there are clothes all over the place and a comic is opened at a universally recognisable spread: the story of *Mickey Mouse*. Slightly isolated in the top right hand corner of this frame which signifies the enclosed world of the two creatures, is a shining red motorbike indicating a possible adventure. The ensuing pages follow the pair as they get up to numerous antics on their newly-found transportation. The bike takes them to diverse parts of their farmyard and through a duck-pond. Here the mice are frowned upon by the other farmyard animals who are frightened by their speed as they send water uncontrollably out of the frame.

Category 2 – Visual narrative techniques: Once the mice are on the open road, the excitement and emotion engendered in the narrative sequence build towards the inevitability of calamity. They wreck the motorbike, damage themselves and have to be administered to by its owner who, surprisingly, does not chastise them but merely keeps them under tight control the next time they venture out. In the final illustration, his complete control of both the mice and the environment is emphasised by the farmer's hand, knee and foot breaking the frame in which the scene is set (fig.18). The abundance of circumstantial detail here renews itself on each reading.

95

Figure 18: in *D'Grisette an D'Choupette um Motorrad* (Theis and Ries, 1995: 21)
A relationship of tight control!

Category 3 – Types of picture book: There is a certain over-the-top quality in this text, evident in the visual portrayal of the characters of the two mice. The bright colours of their garments and the absurdity of their antics suggest 'excess'. They move away from whatever decorum might be attributed to the story, and the tale is brought to a conclusion through measures undertaken by the censorious adult.

Category 4 – Picture book ingredients: Unlike the themes of other texts in this section, the focus here on authoritarian friendship brings together the worlds of adult and child. Both inhabit the real world but often it is children or child-like characters who contribute to the fantasy narrative. In *D'Grisette an D'Choupette um motorrad*, picture book ingredients are fully utilised and crazy ideas lead to trouble which ends in conflict resolution and a more restricted freedom. This is a universal occurrence within the world of child-hood. The linguistic diversity of Luxembourg is reflected in the multilingual text, and such language richesse is an especially significant factor for many children in European countries.

Das Land der Ecken (The land of corners) Austria

Category 1 – Visual Codes: Irene Ulitzka and Gerhard Gepp's picture book is about the acceptance of difference. Stories often start with significant end-papers or important title pages, and this one opens with angular shapes and concludes with circular ones. Their significance emerges as the story pro-gresses. The initial shapes are pastel-shaded triangles with slightly misted edges on one side, denoting the world of corners – but the fuzziness of the one side suggests slight uncertainty.

In the beginning there is the world – a world of seven corners, totally un-inhabited by anything non-angular. Into this world of corners enters some-thing round. Neither the angular child nor triangular cat know what to do with it, so they take it to an adult, who is especially uncertain about this alien shape and takes it to his colleagues. Unable to fit it into their own worldly knowledge, these adults throw the object to the ground, breaking it and making it conform to their own familiar images. After which the older generation depart rapidly, leaving both the child and his pet cat rather dis-turbed, as can be seen by the way that the cat covers his eyes and the boy rests his head on his finger. The two then go off together. They see a balloon in the sky; trees that are round, the round sun, a scooter with round wheels and … a boy with a round face. The two boys have no difficulty in communicating, and go off to play together on a round-wheeled scooter, led by the cat (fig.19). The final endpapers have fuzzy round shapes instead of square ones.

Category 2 – Visual narrative techniques: These fuzzy images of both tri-angles and circles are the essence of this narrative, almost a mirror of each

Figure 19: in *Das Land der Ecken,* (Ulitzka and Gepp, 1993: 24/25)
Childhood acceptance of difference.

child's emotional point of contact. The theme of the story is that even though there may be significant differences in communication, sharing is still possible. Children are often more capable of accepting this than adults because they have less pre-conceived prejudices and may move in less polarised worlds among children of differing lifestyles. A variety of shapes and icons depicting the many circumstantial details which reinforce this theme permeate *Das Land der Ecken*, as do several confrontational images indicated by the positioning of the adults and children.

Category 3 – Types of picture book: This picture book presents a number of different semiotic interpretations of life in the land of corners. If one takes each illustration separately there is very little progression in the picture sequencing and it appears that readers have to work extremely hard to work out the 'indeterminacy' of the story line. Examination of the juxtaposition of images like the cat add a vital cohesive element.

Category 4 – Picture book ingredients: Peter Schneck (in Cotton, 1996) suggests that this secondary world of corners is important because of the difficulty of finding peace and accord within a Europe of so many diverse views. By using a variety of picture book ingredients this Austrian book intimates a possible harmony in the face of these differences.

A ovelha negra (The black sheep) Portugal 99

Category 1 – Visual codes: This book asks readers to consider what would happen when something unfamiliar enters their secure world. Malaquias' story begins early in the morning in the Portuguese countryside, when the sun is about to rise and the sky is dotted with white fluffy clouds. As the narrator looks closely at these clouds, she sees small faces with tiny eyes appearing. They begin to unroll slowly as if they had parachutes and fall to the ground. Suddenly a black sheep descends into this serene world (fig.20) and a question mark leaves readers to consider what might happen next.

Category 2 – Visual narrative techniques: Although written for infants, this narrative has considerable potential for discussing aspects of tolerance with older children. The main characters (sheep) are seen at a distance, thus increasing concern about their role within the story. The serenity of the countryside lulls readers into a false sense of security and doesn't really prepare them for the harsh reality of the intrusion. In its apparent naivety, this little book exposes narrative techniques which establish links between things that are difficult to connect (Iser,1978). Readers are forced to reconsider information they first considered quite straightforward, triggered – as is often the case – by certain emotive semiotic images .

Figure 20: in *A ovelha negra* (Malaquias, 1988 11) – And then?

Category 3 – Types of picture book: The author tells her story in the first person, as if in conversation, stepping 'beyond the boundaries' of the narrative. Then she invites her readers to shape the direction of the story, either alone or in discussion with others; the metafictive relationship between the visual and written texts is crucial.

Category 4 – Picture book ingredients: Acceptance of difference is conveyed in this short text through a number of picture book ingredients which allow the fantasy world to impinge on the lives of its young readers. As the visual tale literally unfolds, the opportunity arises to consider personal relationships and reflect on those of others, perhaps from different cultures.

Starting School – England

Category 1 – Visual codes: Starting School was selected by Margaret Meek (see Cotton, 1996) because it was conceived in school with the help of pupils and reflects the world of school in England, as seen through the eyes of children. A double spread and carefully sectioned pages draw readers into the lives of all who attend Riverside Primary School from the moment they arrive on the first day, some on bikes others in cars and many on foot. The bright profusion of colours in the perceptive illustrations pave the way for an experience that is to be enjoyed! Moving left to right across the page the protagonists meet a cheerful lollipop man, open mouthed and chatty, who is showing children from a variety of ethnic backgrounds across the road. The themes of child to adult and child to child friendship are reinforced.

Category 2 – Visual narrative techniques: The excitement of the children arriving at school is conveyed through minute circumstantial details in a montage of vignettes so typical of Janet Ahlberg's illustrative style. Where to hang coats, where to find the toilets, where to eat, which people are important and to whom – all are details vital for children starting school. The illustrations are interspersed with text, and can be read sequentially or at whichever point of interest catches readers' attention. The story follows children through their first term and concludes with a Christmas play, where the vibrancy of a school production is captured in the diversity of the characters and the warmth of colours used for this traditionally English winter scene.

Category 3 – Types of picture book: An important feature of the metafictive picture book is communication between visual and written text (see Chapter Six). In the Ahlbergs' book, these two elements not only interact but are physically interwoven, almost stepping 'beyond the boundaries' of conventional texts. Readers are drawn into the narrative and can take a personal journey through the book, stopping wherever their interest is held. The text or dialogue alone would not be sufficient to create this adventure; it is the interaction of the perceptive visual and written narratives that allows readers to make this book their own.

Figure 21: in *Starting School* (Ahlberg and Ahlberg, 1990: 25) – United in pride!

Category 4 – Picture book ingredients: Several picture book ingredients contribute to the intertextuality in the denouement of this story. Not only are the well known nativity characters present but parents and teachers also have their place, encircling the angels – the very children who were seen coming to school at the beginning of the book. The expressions on these young faces are shown through the flick of a pencil line or the slight tilt of a head and capture the expressions of children of this age: most are happy, one or two are sad, one has forgotten his costume and one is waving to her mother. The 'Englishness' of this vignette is conveyed in the school scene: the stage, the piano, the teacher turning the pages of music and the faces of the parents united in their cheerfulness and pride on this festive occasion.

It is apparent from this analysis of picture book narratives (further detailed in Cotton, 1997) that the STA framework provides a potential structure for discussing picture book texts which could be used to focus on universal themes likely to permeate any collection of picture books. Bringing together the semiotic focus of a number of picture book researchers into one analytic framework demonstrates Barthes' (1957) theory that 'pictures, like writing require a lexis'. The framework provides a method of evaluating a set of European picture books against a given set of criteria set out in Table 3 (Chapter Six) – a framework which other educationalists can consider and use.

The STA allows for parallels between visual narratives in picture books and is ideal for this collection from member states of the European Union. As each picture book is analysed, it is possible to see the connections readers might make between visual, spoken and written narratives. The static aspects of visual codes that are used visually to describe the *setting* of the books in Category 1 could be equated with descriptive spoken and written language, the active visuals of *story* with active language, and a combination of both with *people*.

An analogy can also be made with written text analysis in that *people* might be seen as what Brown and Yule (1988: 126) call 'theme' – the starting point of an utterance; *setting* as 'rheme' – everything else that follows in a sentence; and *story* as 'staging' – the writer's cognitive structuring. Using the notion of theme as main character means that what the writer puts first (the subject) will influence the interpretation of everything that follows. Visual narrative techniques can thus be seen as part of a wider discourse. The circumstantial details and icons in Category 2 could be seen as further linguistic embellishments, ie the adjectival phrases that enhance a text, while trigger images and cartoon formats could be viewed as devices to move the narrative on, possibly equating with adverbial phrases and clauses.

The majority of picture book ingredients in Category 4 relate to *people* and *story*, with a smaller number included in the *setting* classification. These elements compare with the thematic organisation of a narrative and the author's attempt to relate events meticulously to each other in time (Brown and Yule, 1988: 143). They are the parts of speech and the functions of language that create cohesion. In written text the physical anaphoric and cataphoric make the cohesive links, whereas visual texts provide the opportunities for readers of picture books to make sense of the narrative through their own cohesive acts. It is the types of picture books in Category 3 that they read which enable this interaction and which provide analogies with adult fiction.

Parallels could also be drawn between visual and written stories, so visual analysis could be used with older children to develop their knowledge and understanding of both spoken and written language and also of how narrative works on a number of levels.

The analytical framework seeks to provide a structure whereby the texts can be analysed as material produced for discourse, which enables the mimetic function of messages (discussed in Chapter Six) to go back and forth between picture book and reader. Since children's responses to illustrations are inseparable from their response to text, their thoughts, ideas and reactions often stem from reading pictures. They then draw inferences, putting cause and effect together to form and create the fundamental elements of plot structure. Readers can experience how characters themselves sort out, frequently

104 through fantasy, the difficult experiences of growing up and converting their surroundings into something real and manageable. Thus the secondary worlds of picture books have a great deal to offer but children will only respond to a serious message if the visual narrative is presented honestly and entertainingly. Illustrations such as those in the EPBC that are full of symbolism and use a comic format, can keep children in touch with popular culture.

Thematic analysis highlights the important role that picture books can play in facilitating a wider understanding of Europe, especially by drawing on the universal childhood issues common to all cultures. Visual images in the texts can be seen as clues or symbols to be understood, at first without supportive text, and are all the more powerful because children have to bring their own personal meaning to them. The visual narratives presented are all based on a belief that children want to think as well as be entertained, and that all texts have the capacity to leave images in the mind which allow meaning to grow and develop. Older children are likely to respond to the respect which the authors/illustrators have accorded them and to learn how to read the meaningful messages that the books contain. Finally, modern European picture books can contribute to children's learning of literary as well as cultural conventions that all readers need to be aware of and to operate throughout their lives.

Chapter Eight
European Picture Books and the Curriculum

C hapter Eight draws on the findings from the semiotic text analysis discussed in the previous chapter, and focuses on the linguistic interaction between picture and text. All the EPBC picture books were designed so that the illustrations and written text interact but, as the texts are in a range of European languages, this study has so far focused on the visual storytelling techniques of each one. This chapter outlines some of the ways in which links can be made between the multilingual texts of these narratives, using as exemplars translations or retellings to complement the visual storylines, and suggests how European picture books might be used in the curriculum.

The polysemic nature of the texts is discussed in relation to how certain book-related activities could be used in upper primary classrooms as a means of facilitating understanding of the similarities between languages and cultures and for giving confidence to children who are learning English as an additional language – or the language of the European country in which they have settled. Also considered is how the EPBC can be used to teach literary forms, as the collection enables teachers to place the picture books within a European setting and facilitates close scrutiny of linguistic, literary and cultural elements relating to language, literature and storytelling generally.

Picture Books Sans Frontières has related how philosophers and educationalists have been extolling the value of picture books to learning, since the time of Comenius. Today, picture books are widely used in schools throughout Europe but there has been little exchange of ideas between member states about ways of making the 'travelability' of picture books, mentioned in Chapter Three, a reality. There are many opportunities for European picture books to support educational requirements as well as to teach children about Europe. Using the books would provide an opportunity for the languages and countries of origin to be explored, setting the context for using the EPBC by presenting both a geographic and a linguistic dimension. The stories can then be visually sequenced, discussed and analysed, and literary parallels drawn.

The STA is helpful in planning the use of the EPBC in the classroom. The interplay between picture and text enhances the power of picture books for upper primary children and is a key in developing their understanding of how texts work at a number of levels. The EPBC is characterised by such interplay and older children can learn to interrogate these texts in practical classroom activities. Using books from a variety of cultures shows pupils that teachers respect the language and literature of other cultures. This is an important lesson for all pupils. Refugee or settler children are less likely to feel 'alien' in an environment where no culture or language is felt by the 'mainstream' to be foreign (Pinsent, 1997: 109). In acknowledging the importance of other languages and cultures, teachers help these children to feel that they have an important role to play in the development of intercultural understanding. It is equally valuable for children whose native language is that of the country in which they live to be aware that their mother tongue is not the only language that matters.

Each of the books in the EPBC was originally created for its country of origin but in the collection each offers a wider dimension, of which the author/ illustrator may have been unaware. An approach to using these books has been evolved which immerses teachers into the language and culture of the books while they study the literary forms of each text. It is hoped that this approach will enhance other literary and linguistic understanding and facilitate teaching upper primary pupils more about Europe, its literature and its languages. One EPBC book indicates how all nineteen of them support curriculum requirements: *Kees en Keetje* is used to demonstrate how extension material can be developed, although any of the texts could be equally effective.

106

The Dutch text has been chosen because:

- it has a clear visual narrative structure

- its setting, although universally recognised, makes a number of cultural references

- characterisation develops well, visually

- the theme of the 'ups and downs' of friendship is universal

- many linguistic comparisons can be made between Dutch and English.

The illustrations are crucial: what is difficult to say in words can often be communicated in pictures. The universality of illustrations enables children to appreciate a familiar story in a new way and find deeper layers of meaning. Familiarity with the conventions which communicate meaning allows children to follow complex narrative portrayed in the images. And pictures offer readers a position of power, allowing them to observe the story from different viewpoints and understand how narrative and language work through interaction with the text.

Learning about languages not too different from their own can help pupils to understand more about how language works. Dutch is probably the closest European language to English and has the most similarities. It is not widely spoken outside the Netherlands (although it is very similar to Flemish) but it could extend the linguistic competence of many young learners.

Classroom activities based on *Kees and Keetje* by Jantien Buisman

Story Synopsis

> This is the story of two hedgehogs who have lived together for a long time. They have put up with each other's unpleasant habits of burping or picking their noses, because they love each other.

> One day, however, they become so irritated by each other's habits that they decide to separate. This means they have to divide up all their belongings, which they do not do very sensibly. For example, Kees takes the bed and Keetje the mattress!

> Whenever they pass each other they look the other way but, one day, they meet when each is carrying half of their favourite meal: chips and apple sauce (a children's favourite in the Netherlands). This makes them realise how much they need each other and they decide to become friends again.

107

The following activities all relate to this book. Practical classroom suggestions are made in the left hand columns of each table, with their objectives on the right.

Activity One: introductory discussion

Rationale

Each book in the EPBC can be set within a European context by:

- locating it geographically in relation to the other member states on a map of Europe

- discussing the language spoken, making reference to the influence that surrounding countries may have, eg why a language similar to Dutch is spoken in the Flemish part of Belgium; or the influence of French, German and Italian on the languages spoken in Luxembourg

- sharing any known characteristics relating to culture, literature, food, music etc.

- discussing any interactions pupils may have or have had with the country.

Table 5: Activity One – An introduction to *Kees en Keetje*

Practical Activity	Objectives
Discussion BEFORE 'reading'.	**Focus on the importance of discussion about the book: its title, author, publisher and possible storyline. Particular notice should be paid to the similarities and differences between the Dutch and English languages.**
TITLE: Look at title, together with pictures. *Kees En Keetje* What is it in English? *Kees and Keetje* What helped the translation? eg. picture; two characters; knowledge that characters have names (proper nouns); knowledge that nouns are often joined with and (a conjunction) in book titles	Focus on the similarities with English: phrase structure use of nouns conjunctions punctuation eg upper case 'K' – indicates proper noun
Are there any letter combinations that are different from English? *tje*	Focus on differences eg letter combinations
AUTHOR: Discuss the name: Jantien Buisman Guess the Nationality: Dutch Male or Female? female Are there any letter combinations that are different from English? *tien; uis*	Focus on name and possible pronunciation Introduction to concept of different nationalities Possible clues to gender Common letter strings
PUBLISHER: Name: Uitgeverij De Harmonie Place: Amsterdam Year: 1976 Are these conventions the same in English books? In which country is Amsterdam situated? Are there any letter combinations that are different from English? *uit; rij* Are there any words that are similar to English? Can you come to any conclusions about the Dutch language eg the 'j' features significantly but there are some words that are similar to English (*harmonie*) What is the story likely to be?	Similarities and differences Knowledge of place names/use of upper case Comparisons of technique Geographical reference; locate on map Linguistic comparisons Linguistic reflection Knowledge about: narrative structure, story conventions, universal themes, and importance of titles and illustrations.

Comparisons can also be made between the literary and linguistic similarities and differences of English texts and those of the country in question. Activity One (Table 5) suggests some possible ways in which this could be done with *Kees en Keetje.*

Activity Two: teaching about narrative structure

Rationale

Before any written activity is set for children, objectives need to be established which include a sense of audience and purpose (National Writing Project, 1988). As this book is in Dutch, it is necessary to write an English version (purpose) for children in – in this instance – the UK (audience). Only the synopsis of the story and the pictures are there to help with this task. Specific objectives for Activity Two are set out in Table 6.

The task has been devised to enable teachers and pupils to reflect on how much time needs to be spent on speaking, listening and reading before any writing takes place. Thereafter the stages of writing need to be explored. This involves all the drafting processes plus proof reading (including spelling) before the work is finally presented for publication – and even at this stage more re-reading and discussion might be required.

Activities Three and Four: teaching about linguistic knowledge

Rationale

After the story has been written and the children are thoroughly familiar with the illustrations and narrative structure attention can be paid on the text which accompanies the pictures. The tasks outlined in Tables 7 and 8 deal with the similarities between languages and linguistic knowledge.

Table 6: Activity Two – Kees en Keetje: teaching about narrative structure

Practical Activity	Objectives
1. In groups of 6, form 3 pairs: **A,B,C**. Pair bilingual children with native speakers	Establish narrative framework in 'home groups'
2. Using photocopied storyboards from *Kees and Keetje*: Pair **A** discusses what is happening in each picture of the 'beginning section' Pair **B** discusses what is happening in each picture of the 'middle section' Pair **C** discusses what is happening in each picture of the 'end section'.	Use of National Oracy Project (1991) 'jig-sawing' technique to establish 'expert groups'
3. Each pair **A** now joins another pair **A** Each pair **B** now joins another pair **B** Each pair **C** now joins another pair **C**.	Sharing of expertise
4. In new groups, discuss ideas about each part story. Are there any differences? Does anything need to be changed?	Possible revision of initial ideas
5. Back in original groups of six, discuss the possibilities for a group story: pair **A** writes the beginning, **B** the middle and **C** the end. Talk about ways of linking the three parts.	Share expertise in 'home groups' to establish thematic narrative
6. Split into pairs again and write a sentence (or more) about what is happening in each picture. It should be written as if the story were to accompany the pictures.	Structure of written text and its relationship with visuals
7. In original groups, the whole story is to be read through. Does it make sense? Do the three parts link together? Do changes need to be made?	Revision: revising, re-drafting, proof reading
8. Get together with another group of six and read own story to them/listen to theirs. Try to make at least one positive comment about each story, and one about how it might be improved.	Sharing of narrative: responding to and assessing of written work, making relevant suggestions acting as response partners (National Writing Project 1988)
9. The story is now ready for publication.	
10. When finished, think about how much time was spent **speaking and listening**, how much time **reading**, and how much time was actually spent **writing**.	Summarise skills required

Table 7: Activity Three – *Kees en Keetje*: teaching about linguistic knowledge – similarities between languages

Practical Activity	Objectives
	Focus on similarities between languages makes them appear less alien.
Using the illustrations and knowledge of the story, try to work out the meaning of this Dutch sentence in English:	The previous activity encouraged the text to be guessed from the illustrations and story context.
"*Ze gaven mekaar een dikke kus*" Figure 22 (They gave each other a big kiss)	Here links with English can be made with the written form of *kus*.
Focus on *why* words can be guessed	A further guess might then be made about the word *dikke* (big), and another that they gave each other a big kiss.
	Noun = *kus*: visible similarity to English
	Adjective = *dikke*: visible in picture
	Verb = *gaven*: visible similarity to English
	Article = *een*: implicit in grammatical structure
	Pronoun = Ze: substitute for Kees and Keetje
	mekaa = most difficult word. It can only be guessed from the context of the sentence.

111

Figure 22: Ze gaven mekaar een dikke kus

Table 8: Activity Four – Kees en Keetje: teaching about linguistic knowledge – language structure

Practical Activity

Objectives

Attention to language structure in another language helps focus on one's own.

Refer to translation of the text which accompanies Figure 23.

Comparison of languages:
words learned already: *ze* = pronoun
same in English: *lamp, pan* = noun
similar in English: *bord* = noun
that re-occur: op – *in/on* = preposition
       het/de – the = article

Discussion of similarities and differences:
eg more than one meaning for *op* – the problem of prepositions in transference of languages

het and *de* = definite article: 'the'   Many languages have genders for nouns

Sentence structure:
Discuss why lines two to five do not begin with a capital letter.

Ellipsis: "They put the" is understood and therefore omitted.

Discussion of 'subject-verb-object-adverbial' in these clauses

To be used as an entrée into work related to of parts of speech and functions of language.

Compare sentence by sentence translation from Dutch into English

Make comparisons with the Dutch language – focus on how many words can be recognised and easily translated into English.

Listen to the tape whilst reading the Dutch language alongside the illustrations.

Discuss how much of the text can be understood.

Focus on differences between reading the text and listening to the tape.

Allow comparisons between written and spoken language, discussion on pronunciation of words and relationship with English. Also, difficulties between written and spoken words eg spelling.

Fig. 23:

Ze deden de kap weer op de lamp,	*They put the shade back on the lamp,*
het deksel op de pan,	*the lid back on the pan,*
het kopje op de schotel	*the cup back on the saucer*
de stoffer op het blik	*the brush back in the dustbin*
de schaakstukken op het dambord.	*the chessmen back on the draughts board.*

113

Using the EPBC to teach literary forms

As well as knowing about linguistic and narrative structure, teachers need to be aware of the literary techniques that can be taught through using European picture books, both at their own level and in upper primary classrooms. The visual aspect of picture books is at the heart of *Picture Books Sans Frontières*. This strengthens the impact of the stories and enhances the value of many literary techniques and provides opportunities for older children to understand literary narratives more fully. Just as graphic organisers can aid reading comprehension, the visual art in books can support and illuminate such devices as character development, mood, point of view, irony and satire (Keifer, 1995: 184). The European books included in the EPBC have the ability to heighten children's understanding of important literary elements such as the following:

Characterisation

Where characters in literature have numerous facets – which generally develop as a story progresses – these are portrayed en route. We saw in Chapter Seven how illustrators can convey the development of their characters: the frightened *Toffle* who gains confidence once he has reason to be brave, or the self-confident *Groucho* who experiences one or two setbacks which cause him to question his bravado before returning to his protective home environment. Comparisons are possible with all the European protagonists in the EPBC – they either grow (like *Grandpa*) or deteriorate (like the *Fat King*). Discussion of this progression of character development within the narrative will extend children's comprehension of visual characterisation.

Climax

The point in the story where the outcome is decided is usually the moment of greatest tension and the crucial element on which narrative depends. In *Une nuit, un chat...* it is *Groucho's* confrontation with the sewer rat; in *Grisette and Choupette* it is the crashing of the red motorcycle; in *A ovelha negra* it is the entry of the black sheep; for the boy in *Das Land der Ecken* it is breaking the round object which does not conform to his country's culture. Central elements of tension, crucial to any story-line, are an integral part of all the books in the European collection and provide opportunities for analysing the organisation and structure of texts

Elaboration and Detail

Specific attention to fine detail helps identify the unique qualities of characters, setting and plot. This will facilitate deeper understanding and appreciation of the story. The setting of *Kan du vissla Johanna*, for example, with its focus on fine lines and shapes, creates an environment which alludes to the Swedish culture and its treatment of old people while simultaneously suggesting an air of mischief in the protagonists. The details of character and setting in *Katie Morag and the new pier* open a window onto life in a Scottish fishing village and its inhabitants, whereas *Starting School* presents snapshots which encapsulate the 'Englishness' of its setting with its minute vignettes of English life. The fine detail in *El guardián del olvido*, on the other hand, takes the reader into a surreal world enhanced with references to Spanish culture and contrasts dramatically with the minutia in the illustrations of the creatures in *Mosekonens Bryg*, Denmark's earthy world.

Foreshadowing

This helps readers to anticipate coming events and guess what will happen next. In *Das Land der Ecken* the prediction that the round object might be broken is facilitated through the detailed expression of the characters and the directionality of their movements, and so is the possibility of meeting and going off with a round-headed child. In *Hallo, kleiner Wal* the appearance of the whale is foreshadowed in a sequence of predictable events. Similarly *Grisette's and Choupette's* crash comes as no surprise. These predictive elements of visual texts, so crucial to early reading development and understanding narrative, are also used to great effect in more sophisticated novels to give readers insights into possible developments. Using sophisticated picture book texts to analyse these strategies with older primary children can facilitate their later comprehension of novels they read at secondary level.

Irony

The device of using actions or words that are the opposite of what is expected is a traditional literary quality in picture books for older children. The farmer who administers to the needs of *Grisette and Choupette* after their motorcycle accident, for example, is expected to chastise the young mice but instead he allows them out on his bike again – but this time under strict supervision! The visual image here is very forceful. The irony in *Mosekonens Bryg* is a little more subtle. Traditionally one would expect the bringers of Spring to be bright and cheerful, happily injecting new life to the countryside. But here are the marsh people brewing their beer, as a fore-runner to what they feel is necessary for enjoyment in the lighter months of the year!

Tone or Mood

The implied feeling or attitude of the author/illustrator comes through in many of the EPBC books. In *Lotje is jarig* for example, illustrator Lieve Baeten creates a colourful and warm environment in which to place her apprentice witch. Through tone of colours and delicacy of brush-strokes, she creates a mood which reflects the light-heartedness of Lotje on her birthday. In contrast, Alfonso Ruano produces a sombre mood with illustrations that depict uncertainty in tone for *El guardián del olvido*. Blues, blacks and browns convey a message of mystery and intrigue which pervades the book. And the watery colours of *Cantre'r Gwaelod* set the tone for an enigmatic tale of a city submerged beneath the sea.

Parody

The humorous imitation of a well-known work or form can be seen in *Un jour mon Prince viendra*. Traditionally, the prince is handsome and the young girl beautiful but here the images are very different – the prince is a rather rotund baker and the prospective princess a brash and aggressive witch! Parody also features in *War and Peas*, where the serious nature of the continuing friction between Great Britain and Northern Ireland is depicted in allegorical fashion, the richer country being seen as having an over-large King who governs a land of plenty depicted in exaggerated images of food and drink, while the poor kingdom is governed by a gaunt and fading lion.

115

Point of View

The perspective taken by the author in *A ovelha negra* is that of a dreamer who has only to look up at the sky to imagine the clouds transforming. This fantasy is transmitted to readers, who are allowed to dream also, but when an element of conflict in the form of a black sheep enters this peaceful world, the author hands over for the readers to complete. They can either remain within the world of fantasy or, in discussion, make analogies with real-life situations. *La bambina che non voleva andare a dormire* presents the viewpoint of the child. Anna doesn't want to go to bed and recounts her story personally, seeing herself participating in a dominant position in every tale her father tells. The readers' role is to empathise with Anna's point of view and make relevant forays into their own fantasies.

Satire

Criticism of social or human weaknesses, often through exaggeration, is a feature of books based on universal themes that relates to sayings such as 'Pride comes before a fall' (Wales); 'Too much of a good thing' (Greece); or 'If at first you don't succeed … ' (Ireland). Intriguingly, food is a feature of all three books and an excess of it is seen in many cultures as a sign of human weakness. A Welsh king loses his city because he is too proud to leave the banqueting hall while his subjects are feasting. The Greek story-spinner eats so many sweets that he longs for something savoury. And it is the Irish Saint Patrick who tries many times to help Crom Dubh to believe and, finally, succeeds.

Teaching literary forms through European picture books can be done by concentrating on specific aspects of texts. The preceding discussion on individual books will meet many curriculum needs including: an analysis of character and plot, organisation and structure, argument and viewpoint, and relationships to other texts. By developing their critical responses, children are helped to make connections between books. Oral and written activities require pupils to make critical and imaginative responses to aspects of literature and to evaluate the texts they read, referring to relevant passages or episodes to support their opinions. Focus on the story structure, characterisation, setting and themes of European picture books facilitates teaching compositional skills by drawing on pupils' knowledge of spoken language and reading as a model or stimulus for writing and for increasing their awareness of differences between written and spoken language. Hearing, discussing, re-telling, recounting and describing events is instrumental in developing pupils' enthusiasm for reading and allows them to listen attentively to and participate effectively in discussions. By using the EPBC teachers can gain insight into how international comparisons can inform their teaching and help them to evaluate texts critically.

Chapter Nine
European Picture Books and the
National Literacy Strategy

The National Literacy Strategy operating in British primary classrooms is an ideal scenario for using the EPBC materials in schools. This chapter suggests ways of using the EPBC materials for iniatives such as the Literacy Hour, officially introduced into primary schools in England in 1998. It presents an example of the EPBC's use in upper primary classrooms over one term, to both implement a European dimension and support the text, sentence and word level requirements of the English framework. It also suggests how other lessons can be planned and developed around the EPBC or other relevant picture books.

The National Literacy Strategy (NLS) 'range' for Year 5 (10 year olds), term 3, requires teachers to use a range of stories from a variety of cultures and traditions (NLS, 1998:48). The EPBC is particularly supportive in meeting the requirements set out in the NLS framework, where:

at 'text' level pupils should be taught:

1. to investigate a range of texts from different cultures, considering patterns of relationships, social customs, attitudes and beliefs:

    – identify these features by reference to the text

    – consider and evaluate these features in relation to their own experience

2. to identify the point of view from which a story is told and how this affects the reader's response

3. to change point of view, e.g. tell about incident or describe a situation from the point of view of another character or perspective

4. to read, rehearse and modify performance of poetry

7. to write from another character's point of view e.g. retelling an incident in letter form

8. to record predictions, questions, reflections while reading, e.g. through use of a reading journal

9. to write in the style of the author, e.g. writing to complete a section, resolve a conflict; writing additional dialogue, new chapter

10. to write discursively about a novel or story, e.g. to describe, explain, or comment upon it

17. to draft and write individual, group or class letters for real purposes, eg put forward a point of view, comment on an emotive issue, protest; to edit and present in finished state

19. to construct an argument in note form or full text to persuade others of a point of view.

at 'sentence' level pupils should be taught:

1. to secure the basic conventions of standard English:

    – agreement between nouns and verbs

    – consistency of tense and subject

2. to understand how writing can be adapted for different audiences and purposes, e.g. by changing vocabulary and sentence structures

3. to search for, identify and classify a range of prepositions...

7. to use connectives to link clauses within sentences and to link sentences in longer texts.

at 'word' level pupils should be taught:

3. spelling strategies ... using visual skills, e.g. recognising common letter strings and checking critical features

8. to identify everyday words such as spaghetti, bungalow, boutique which have been borrowed from other languages, and to understand how this might give clues to spelling

12. to use dictionaries efficiently to explore spellings, meanings, derivations, e.g. by using alphabetical order, abbreviations, definitions with understanding. (NLS, 1998: 48, 49)

To enhance children's literary and linguistic understanding optimally when using the European picture book texts, there follows a six week plan devised to support Year Five, term three, of the National Literacy Strategy with a 'focus on fiction'. Its rationale is based on the preceding chapters of *Picture Books Sans Frontières* and draws on the analysis of the visual narratives set out in Chapter Seven. Although the activities relate to particular books, all can be adapted for any of the EPBC material or other suitable European picture books.

Week 1: People

VEM ska trösta knyttet? (Finland)
Une nuit, un chat... (France)
La bambina che non voleva andare a dormire (Italy)
Un jour mon Prince viendra (Belgium – French)
Lotje is jarig (Belgium – Flemish)

■ MONDAY: *VEM ska trösta knyttet? (Finland)*
Shared text work (whole class)

Characterisation
Use OHT of fig. 3; based on discussion in Chapter Seven:

How would you describe Toffle?
Why?
What evidence is there in the illustrations?
How does the illustrator convey this?
Which visual codes does she use (ie position, size, shape, colour etc see STA Table 3)
Does she use any visual narrative techniques (eg. trigger images) to give clues about the story?

Gradually build up a picture of who the class think Toffle is and what his role will be in the story.

119

Additional discussion
Toffle appears to frightened of the dark.
Have you ever been frightened of anything?
Why?
How did you get over it?
Could you give Toffle any advice?
How might you help younger children to get over their fears?
Do you know any other books that are concerned with being frightened or lonely?
eg *The owl who was afraid of the dark* (Jill Tomlinson); *It's too frightening for me* (Jan Mark).
Did they help you to overcome your fears?
Why do you think that was?
Discuss the importance of intertextuality when we read ie we link previous experience of reading to what we are currently reading;
Are there any clues in the illustrations which indicate that Toffle might not be English?
What are they?
What do you know about Finland?
Where is it?

Which language/s are spoken there?
What is the climate like?
How might this affect Finnish people?
Could this have anything to do with why Toffle is afraid of the dark?

Shared word and sentence work (whole class)

Focus on descriptive language

Divide board or flip chart into two

Side 1

*   Brainstorm on all the words, phrases and sentences that the children use to describe Toffle (circle all the descriptive language ie the adjectives)

*   Make an alphabetic list of these adjectives; look for similarities within spellings eg frightened/scared (verbs converted into adjectives)

Side 2

*   Class to pick out the language they like best and begin to create a class character description of Toffle.

Compare with an English character description eg Stig or Barney in *Stig of the dump* by Clive King.

120

Guided text work; independent word/sentence level work

Focus on use of descriptive language and on point of view

Group One: Discuss POV **with teacher** – look at other characters in the book – describe them, consider how they might see Toffle. Create a character 'dossier' from the POV of the other characters.

Group Two: Newspaper report – create headlines and outline of story eg 'Frightened Finn found in dark' (discuss alliteration).

Group Three: Place an advert in lonely hearts club magazine from Toffle, or create the message that he puts in a bottle because he wants to find a friend.

Group Four: Police WANTED poster – this could be devised by his mum and dad because they want to find him.

Group Five: Letters from readers to their friends describing Toffle and discussing how to cheer him up, maybe by suggesting books for him to read.

Plenary: reviewing, reflecting, consolidating

So who is Toffle? How do different people see him?

- POV other characters
- POV newspaper reporter
- POV Toffle
- POV Police
- POV readers

Discuss: the different uses of language in each writing style;
the proportion of nouns, verbs, adjectives, adverbs used for descriptions;
the characteristics of descriptive language.

The format for each week should use the visuals as stimuli for descriptive language in the same way, but development of the group work will vary and so will the plenary feedback. Teachers will need to be familiar with the relevant sections in Chapter Seven and the visual codes and narratives that are discussed for each text.

■ TUESDAY: *Une nuit, un chat... (France)*

Shared text work (whole class)

Characterisation

Use OHT of fig. 4, based on discussion in Chapter Seven:

121

How would you describe Groucho? Why?
What evidence is there in the illustrations?
How does the illustrator convey this?
Which visual codes does he use?
Does he use any visual narrative techniques to give clues about the story?

(Gradually build up a picture of Groucho and his role in the story.)

Additional discussion

Is Groucho very different from Toffle?
How does the illustrator convey Groucho's bright and chirpy attitude to life?
Why does he use animals rather than humans?
What do we call this?
What does 'anthropomorphism' mean?
Can you guess from any parts of the word?
What is 'personification'?
Does this happen more in picture books than in longer novels?
Can you think of other books where this occurs? eg *The piggy book* by Anthony Browne.
Are there any clues in the illustrations which indicate that Groucho might come from France?
What are they?

Shared word and sentence work (whole class)
Focus on descriptive language

Divide board or flip chart into two

Side 1

- Brainstorm all the words, phrases, sentences the children use to describe Groucho (circle all the descriptive language ie adjectives and adjectival phrases)

- Make an alphabetic list of adjectival phrases; look for similarities in the structure of the phrases eg 'happy as a sandboy'; 'bright as a button'; note or suggest similes and metaphors.

Side 2

- Class to pick out the language they like best and begin to create a class character description of Groucho, or a poem about him (possibly an acrostic).

What parts of speech do they include? Circle nouns and verbs in other colours.

Guided text work; independent word/sentence level work
Focus on use of descriptive language/point of view

Group One: Look at the double page spread of the sewer rat.
Discuss how the illustrator has used colour in this scene and write down as many words as possible that describe the rat and what he is doing.
Create a WARNING poster, using descriptive words/the imperative form of verbs.

Group Two: Look at page one of the book. Discuss POV of the parents **with teacher**.
Contrast their thoughts about Groucho going out alone with those of Groucho himself. Create a chart of the similarities and differences of their opinions. Look for synonyms and antonyms.

Group Three: Scan the visual storyline of the book.
Jot down all the prepositions that indicate where Groucho is situated on each page.
Write a short poem, beginning each line with a preposition eg:

In doorway his parents ...
On the roof Groucho was ...
Under the stars he ...

Group Four: Write a paragraph containing 6-12 simple sentences describing Groucho.
Use appropriate connectives to make these into 3-6 complex or compound sentences.

Group Five: Brainstorm any words the children know which might come from French.

Why are fête, rendezvous, chauffeur, casserole, biscuit, spelled and pronounced as they are?

Look up these words in a dictionary to see how the derivation of each is shown.

Use the dictionary to find the origins of other words such as: church (Germanic); chaos (Greek); champagne (French).

Plenary: reviewing, reflecting, consolidating

The use of language

*   Contrasting language: synonyms/antonyms
*   The power of language: imperatives
*   Prepositions
*   Simple, complex, compound sentences
*   Etymology of words

■ WEDNESDAY: *La bambina che non voleva andare a dormire (Italy)*

Shared text work (whole class)

Characterisation

Use OHT of fig. 5, based on discussion in Chapter Seven:

How would you describe Anna? Why?

What evidence is provided in the illustrations?

How does the illustrator convey this information?

Which visual codes does he use?

Does he use any visual narrative techniques to give clues about the story?

(Gradually build up a picture of Anna and her relationship with her father.)

Additional discussion

Is Anna very different from Toffle and Groucho?

Is it possible to find out what she is really like?

Do we have any detailed pictures of her?

Why do you think the illustrator always shows her in different relationships with her father?

How does the illustrator communicate that Anna is controlling her father?

Why do you think he does this?

Why does Anna try to put off going to bed?

Many of the illustrations contain images that are known throughout Europe (such as Mickey Mouse) but are there any clues to indicate that Anna is Italian?

Shared word and sentence work (whole class)
Focus on descriptive language
Divide board or flip chart into two

Side 1:

- Brainstorm all the words, phrases and sentences the children use to describe Anna and her activities.

- Highlight in different colours all the nouns, verbs, adjectives, adverbs they use.

Side 2:

- Class to pick out the language they like best and begin to create a class character description of Anna's relationship with her father.

How does this language differ from the character studies of Toffle and Groucho?

Guided text work; independent word/sentence level work
Focus on use of descriptive language and point of view

Group One: Anna's mother has gone away for a while. Send a telegram to her from Anna's father, explaining what Anna is doing at bed-time and how he feels (economy of language).

Group Two: Scan *La bambina che non voleva andare a dormire* and see how many of the characters that appear in Anna's stories are familiar to you. Create you own bed-time story that Anna could use.

Group Three: Scan the visual storyline of the book **with teacher**.
Discuss all the active verbs that describe Anna's actions in fig.5.
In pairs, pupils re-tell Anna's actions in the past, present and future tenses. Discuss how these tenses are formed.
Select suitable computer fonts to re-tell Anna's tales in the three tenses
eg *past*, present, future.

Group Four: Create a short dialogue between Anna and her father, in which Anna is trying to persuade him that she really doesn't need to go to bed.
Use phrases such as: 'surely'; 'it wouldn't be very difficult ...' etc (NLS, 1998: 49).
Act it out in the plenary, if you wish.

Group Five: Draft an outline of a magazine article about children using delaying tactics because they don't want to go to bed.

Plenary: reviewing, reflecting, consolidating
The use of language
- Economy of language
- Narrative voice
- Past, present and future tenses
- Persuasive dialogue
- Journalists' jargon

■ THURSDAY: *Un jour mon Prince viendra (Belgium – French)*
Shared text work (whole class)

Characterisation
Use OHT of fig. 6, based on discussion in Chapter Seven:
How would you describe Marguerite? Why?
What evidence is there in the illustrations?
How does the illustrator convey this?
Which visual codes does she use?
Does she use any visual narrative techniques to give clues about the story?

(Gradually build up a picture of Marguerite's domineering behaviour.)

Additional discussion:
Is Marguerite a sympathetic character?
Do you like her?
Why/why not?
Marguerite's character is part of a fairy-tale parody,
why do you think this is?
How does this story differ from traditional fairy-tales?

Shared word and sentence work (whole class)
Focus on descriptive language
Divide board or flip chart into two

Side 1

- Brainstorm on all the words, phrases and sentences the children use to describe Marguerite.

- Compare these with the descriptive language used in previous character studies. Is the characterisation more negative?

- Highlight the most powerful words that the children use.

- Discuss parallels with the three witches speech in Macbeth ...

125

Double, double toil and trouble;
Fire burn and cauldron bubble.

Fillet of a fenny snake,
In the cauldron boil and bake;
Eye of newt, and toe of frog,
Wool of bat, and tongue of dog,
Adder's fork, and blind-worm's sting,
Lizard's leg, and howlet's wing,
For a *charm* of powerful trouble,
Like a hell-broth boil and bubble.

Double, double toil and trouble;
Fire burn and cauldron bubble.   (Act IV, Scene I)

Side 2

• Use Shakespeare's verse as a model for a modern day piece, written from the POV of Marguerite who is trying to cast a spell in order to create a Prince Charming.

Guided text work; independent word/sentence level work
Focus on use of descriptive language and point of view

Group One: Look at the 'shape' of Shakespeare's verse and the way he uses rhyme.
Create a modern day spell for Marguerite which she could use to conjure up a prince of your choice. Who would it be?

Group Two: Highlight all the instances of alliteration in Shakespeare's verse.
Look carefully at fig. 6. and jot down as many words as you can to describe Marguerite.
In different colours highlight pairs of words with the same initial consonant.
Write a short verse using alliteration to describe Marguerite.

Group Three: Make a list of all the stories you know about witches eg *The trouble with Mum* by Babette Cole; *The worst witch* by Jill Murphy; *The Witches* by Roald Dahl.
Write a rhyming couplet about each.
Now do the same for Marguerite.
Are there any attributes that all have in common?

Group Four: *Charm*: discuss duality of meaning (and its role within 'parody') **with teacher**.
Why is the fairytale prince called 'Charming'?
Why does Marguerite need to create a 'charm' to conjure up her prince?
Is Marguerite, herself, charming?

126

Is this 'play on words' used in any other stories that you know? eg *The dearest boy in all the world* (Ted van Lieshout, Turton and Chambers, 1988)

Create your own charm for something you really want, trying to use both Shakespeare's verse and a 'play on words' to help you.

Group Five: Look carefully at the last few pages of *Un jour mon Prince viendra*.

Does Marguerite change at all?

Does she find her Prince?

Who do you think he is?

Is there a moral to this tale?

Write an article for the front page of Marguerite's local newspaper:

'Terrifying witch meets her Prince Charming – local girl makes good'.

Plenary: reviewing, reflecting, consolidating

The use of language

- Rhyme and rhythm
- Alliteration
- Rhyming Couplets
- Duality of meaning
- Tabloid jargon

127

FRIDAY: *Lotje is jarig (Belgium – Flemish)*

Shared text work (whole class)

Characterisation

Use OHT of fig. 7, based on discussion in Chapter Seven:

How would you describe Lotje? Why?

What evidence is there in the illustrations?

How does the illustrator convey this?

Which visual codes does she use?

Does she use any visual narrative techniques to give clues about the story?

(Gradually build up a picture of Lotje's carefree existence.)

Additional discussion

Are witches always portrayed in picture books in the same way?

How are Lotje and Marguerite different?

Do you like Lotje?

Why/why not?

What might be special about a witch like Lotje having a birthday?

Shared word and sentence work (whole class)
Focus on descriptive language
Divide board or flip chart into two

Side 1

• Brainstorm on all the words, phrases and sentences the children use to describe Lotje. Don't forget that it is her birthday.

• Compare these descriptive terms with the descriptive language used to describe Marguerite.

Even though both books are about witches and come from Belgium they are quite different in tone. Try to focus on the differences between the two linguistic characterisations.

Side 2

• Use some of the descriptive language to create the verse for a personalised birthday card to Lotje..

Guided text work; independent word/sentence level work
Short friendship activities

Group One: Make up some magic words like Lotje's 'Hocus Pocus Pompelmoes' and use them to create you own spell for having a great birthday. Think carefully about the rhyme and rhythm of your language.

Group Two: Make a birthday card for Lotje, using Microsoft Publisher. Select appropriate illustrations and language, perhaps using alliteration, metaphors or similes.

Group Three: Lotje lives in a tree house with the moon and stars to enhance her magical night-time existence. Design your favourite type of house and write a short paragraph about it to publish in a glossy magazine. Take care with your descriptive language!

Group Four: Read '*The backward spell*' (Chapter One: *Simon and the witch* by Margaret Stuart Barry). Look carefully at all the dialogue and select parts of it which could be used as a radio play to present to your class.

Group Five: Discuss **with teacher** the fact that all the books this week have looked at how different characters react to the dark. Briefly summarise each character's feelings about the dark. Are there differences across cultures? How have the illustrators shown this? Do these books tell you anything about individual cultures? Make a grid to show the main characteristics of each protagonist.

Plenary: reviewing, reflecting, consolidating

The use of language links with previous sessions

- Rhyme and rhythm
- Alliteration, metaphors and similes
- Descriptive language
- Dialogue
- Cultural comparisons.

As the detailed activities for week one demonstrate, the EPBC can alert pupils to the ways visual codes and techniques are used by illustrators to explore characterisation. The visual narratives also allow for cultural comparisons within the framework of the National Literacy Strategy.

This approach to using the EPBC over one week can be developed for the Literacy Hour in subsequent weeks. Further sessions can also be created by using as a template the activities set out in Chapter Eight concerning: (i) ways of introducing the books (Activity 1, Table 5); (ii) teaching about narrative structure (Activity 2, Table 6); (iii) teaching about linguistic knowledge (Activities 3 and 4, Tables 7 and 8); and (iv) teaching about literary forms.

Week 2: Setting

Any of the following books could be used to focus on the cultural settings of picture book narratives. There is a detailed analysis of each in Chapter Seven:

129

> *Kan du vissla Johanna* (Sweden)
> *Katie Morag and the new pier* (Scotland)
> *El guardián del olvido* (Spain)
> *Mosekonens Bryg* (Denmark)
> *Naomh Pádraig agus Crom Dubh* (Ireland)
> *Cantre'r Gwaelod* (Wales)

Week 3: Story

All the narratives presented in these picture books facilitate focus on the visual storytelling techniques that illustrators use and are discussed in Chapter Seven:

> *Kees en Keetje* (Netherlands)
> *War and Peas* (Northern Ireland)
> *The story-spinner meets the sugar-wizard* (Greece)
> *Hallo, kleiner Wal* (Germany)
> *D'Grisette an D'Choupette um motorrad* (Luxembourg)
> *Das Land der Ecken* (Austria)
> *A ovelha negra* (Portugal)
> *Starting School* (England)

During weeks four, five and six the books already used can be revisited with a focus on: relationships; social customs, attitudes and beliefs; and extended writing.

Week 4: Relationships

	between:
VEM ska trösta knyttet?	child/child
Une nuit, un chat....	parent/child
La bambina che non voleva andare a dormire	parent/child
Un jour mon Prince viendra	adult/adult
Lotje is jarig	child/adults

Week 5: Social customs, attitudes and beliefs

	towards:
Kan du vissla Johanna	death
Katie Morag and the new pier	change
El guardián del olvido	identity
Mosekonens Bryg	coming of Spring
Naomh Pádraig agus Crom Dubh	religion
Cantre'r Gwaelod	pride

Week 6: Extended Writing

Although the Literacy Hour provides opportunities for pupils to focus on the technicalities of written expression, the limit of one hour restricts opportunities for extended writing. The final week in this European programme allows pupils to consolidate their learning by undertaking longer periods of writing. The picture book narratives suggested as a stimulus for this work mirror the requirements of a particular term in the National Literacy Strategy and encourage focus on the literary forms discussed in Chapter Eight which can be widely applied in primary classrooms across Europe.

	Style/Purpose	Literary Form
Kees en Keetje	argument	tone or mood
War and Peas	point of view	parody
The story-spinner meets the sugar-wizard	news report	satire
Hallo, kleiner Wal	discursive	foreshadowing
D'Grisette an D'Choupette um motorrad	protest	irony
Das Land der Ecken	persuasive	climax
A ovelha negra	emotive issue	point of view
Starting School	diary	elaboration/ detail

This chapter indicates how the EPBC can be used to implement the requirements of the 1998 National Literacy Strategy required in schools in the UK. Although the activities for the first week of the six-week programme have been set out in detail, they can be used together with discussions in Chapter Seven and the focus on linguistic analysis and literary forms in Chapter Eight to provide a framework for developing 'personalised' sessions to suit individual classes and pupils in the following weeks. In addition to the books selected for inclusion in the EPBC, a teachers' resource book has been created by European colleagues (Cotton, 1996b) which includes translations and re-tellings of the stories in English, plus additional activities for using with the books.

Working with the EPBC and exploiting the visual narratives of the books can facilitate a European dimension in primary classrooms which is sadly lacking in the UK, while at the same meeting curriculum demands. If upper primary pupils can identify with the universal childhood themes presented in the texts, they will begin to see that authors and illustrators throughout Europe all use similar linguistic and literary conventions to communicate their stories. Once they understand this, children should not only feel more secure within their own culture but also be more accepting of the similarities and differences which exist in others'.

131

Chapter Ten
Conclusion

Running through *Picture Books Sans Frontières* are two main strands. One is an exploration of how a European Picture Book Collection can facilitate a European dimension in children's education. The other is the support offered by the EPBC for teaching language and literature in the primary curriculum. These two concepts have been brought together in the belief, shared by participants in the Symposium at which the EPBC began, that much can be learned about other nations through the universal themes that permeate contemporary European fiction. Adults in England may take little interest in picture books published on the Continent but they cannot deny that children throughout the European Community have many common shared experiences. Stories can help create empathy and understanding but European stories will only be systematically used in UK schools and become instruments of change if they can also meet the statutory requirements of the country's education system.

133

Picture Books Sans Frontières sets out to show how the two strands can support one another. It relates how and why the European Picture Book Collection (EPBC) was created and then provides a semiotic text analysis (STA) framework which can be applied to each book so as to provide detailed examples of materials suitable to teach language and literature from a European perspective. The enthusiasm, expertise and advice of European colleagues made it possible to develop a collection of European picture books for this project, with funding from the European Commission. The picture books chosen address the universal childhood theme of *friendship* – a theme with which children throughout Europe can identify. The loneliness of *Toffle* until he finds a friend; *Berra's* need to befriend a grandfather; or the coming together of two boys from utterly different visual worlds as friends, allow children to empathise with childhood characters from other countries who share similar fears, longings and conflicts. While there are undeniable cultural differences among the member states, it is the similarities which these picture books reflect that will help children to begin to see themselves as Europeans.

When the semiotic framework (STA) is applied to each text the resulting analysis produces evidence of the visual similarities and possible interpretations that can be made by young European readers. In addition, the STA focuses on specific visual elements within the narratives that parallel written texts and thus provides a more concrete link for extension activities in school, and in the UK especially for the literacy strategy. Because the EPBC can respond to curriculum requirements it can be used to assist teachers to develop the knowledge and understanding they need in order to secure pupils' progress in language and literacy. Similarly, teachers can enhance their own literary and linguistic skills as they support the National Literacy Strategy. This book shows them how the EPBC texts can be used to focus on character, setting, narrative structure, grammatical terminology and linguistic knowledge. A clear visual narrative structure is essential to initial understanding of story – after which analysis and interaction with the written text becomes possible. The interplay between the visual and written allows for discussion of linguistic terminology and functions.

The project described in *Picture Book Sans Frontières* is unique. It began from personal observation of the interaction between trainee teachers and children using pictures books together in several European schools. Linking these interactions to professional and theoretical knowledge about language and learning led to a broader concept of teaching language and literature and a hypothesis that upper primary school children can learn something about Europe by being immersed in the linguistic worlds of European picture books – a hypothesis which I have attempted to substantiate in this book.

134

Pedagogical innovation doesn't just happen. An investigation is needed into the ways in which schools can implement directives across the whole educational spectrum. Even though the historic development of the picture book in Europe since the 17th Century shows that educationalists have regarded such books as instrumental to the learning process, their potential still does not appear to have been realised in terms of European awareness. A good deal more needs to be done. The EPBC is only a beginning – there are at least four paths to pursue if we are to extend children's understanding of their European peers through the project.

- An in-depth study is needed into the value of the work of translators such as Anthea Bell, and their contribution to the 'Europeaness' of the UK book market.

- The English initiatives need to be replicated or revised across Europe. Eminent European colleagues involved in this study have already demonstrated a perceived need to create materials which would help teachers in their countries to implement a European dimension in primary classrooms. So far materials have mainly been developed for use in English schools but similar work undertaken in other member states would enable more detailed comparison and analysis from which all the countries would ultimately benefit.

- The semiotic text analysis of the visual narratives in the EPBC shows how a universality of themes allows parallels to be drawn between European texts. Again, this has only been done in one country and needs to be applied in other member states so that the effectiveness of the STA can be compared and evaluated.

- The true value of the EPBC material needs to be ascertained by trialling it with children and teachers. This would require three things: firstly, appropriate funding, secondly, the 'know-how' in terms of literary expertise and European knowledge and, thirdly and probably the most difficult, teachers need to be convinced that their pupils would benefit from understanding more about Europe.

In addition to the visual enhancement which texts such as those in the EPBC can bring to children's awareness of narrative structure, there are advantages in using picture books which originate in all the countries of the European Union. Familiarising children with this richesse can help them realise that there are many things which are similar or common all through Europe. Understanding this principle contributes to a sympathetic view of the countries and a shift away from xenophobia and towards harmony. Differences highlighted in the books can help children appreciate the many ways of living, and that each individual country has its own language and culture which enriches the lives of those who are part of it. And for teachers, gaining insight into the visual and linguistic practices in other countries will at the very least aid their ability to observe and reflect upon their own language and culture.

135

I hope that *Picture Books Sans Frontières* has whetted your appetite for European visual narratives. I believe that these picture book texts can do much to give young children throughout Europe greater understanding about each other. I have indicated how we might further implement a European dimension in education and enhance children's learning. The project I began in 1996 has become the joint responsibility of colleagues across the European Union. It began with the sharing of knowledge about children's literature and especially picture books across the EU, and it is now moving towards a structured programme and development of materials which will help educationalists in all European member states to facilitate a greater European awareness in upper primary classrooms. Once children feel secure within their own culture, they are more able to accept the similarities and differences which exist in others and develop a sense of their own national identity and of what it means to be European.

Bibliography

Anagnostopoulos, V.D. (1996) 'Children's Literature in Greece', in P. Hunt (ed.) *International Companion Encyclopedia of Children's Literature*, London: Routledge

Ariés, P. (1973) *Centuries of Childhood*, Harmondsworth: Penguin

Arnheim, R. (1969) *Film as Art*, London: Faber and Faber

Arnheim, R. (1974) *Art and Visual Perception: A Psychology of the Creative Eye*, Berkeley: University of California Press

Baddeley, P. and Eddershaw, C. (1994) *Not So Simple Picture Books*, Stoke on Trent: Trentham

Baker, C.D. and Freebody, P. (1989) *Children's First School Books*, Oxford: Blackwell

Barthes, R. (1957) *Mythologies,* London: Jonathan Cape

Barthes, R. (1974) *S/Z*, New York: Hill and Wang

Beernaert, Y., Van Dijk, H., Sander, T. (1993) *The European Dimension in Teacher Education*, Brussels: ATEE

Benton, M. and Fox, G. (1985) *Teaching Literature Nine to Fourteen*, Oxford: Oxford University Press

Bettelheim, B. (1976) *The Uses of Enchantment: The Meaning and Importance of Fairy Tales*, London: Penguin

Binder, L. (1996) 'Children's Literature in Austria', in P. Hunt (ed.) *International Companion Encyclopedia of Children's Literature*, London: Routledge

Blonsky M. (ed.) (1985) *On Signs*, Oxford: Blackwell

Brennan, G. (1996) 'Coming Across', in the *Times Education Supplement* (March 8th: VIII, 1996)

Bromley, H. (1996) 'Spying on picture books: exploring intertextuality with young children', in V. Watson and M. Styles (eds.) *Talking Pictures*, London: Hodder and Stoughton

Brown, G. and Yule, G. (1988) *Discourse Analysis,* Cambridge: Cambridge University Press

Chambers, A. (1994) Unpublished group presentation at conference: *Introducing European Children's Books in Translation*, London: Roehampton Institute

Chambers, A. (1995) 'European books in translation', unpublished paper presented at conference: *Introducing European Children's Books in Translation*, London: Roehampton Institute

Chambers, A. (1996) 'Introduction' in J. Linders and M. De Sterk (eds.) *Behind the Story*, Amsterdam: Ministerie van de Vlaamse Gemeenschap Administratie Cultuur

Coghlan, V. (1996) 'Picture Books' in V. Coghlan and C. Keenan (eds.) *The Big Guide to Irish Children's Books*, Dublin: Irish Children's Book Trust

Comenius, J.A. (1968) *Orbis Pictus* (Facsimile of the English edition of 1659), Oxford: Oxford University Press

Commission of the European Union (1993) *Green Paper on the European Dimension of Education*, Brussels: Commission of the European Communities

Cotton, P. (ed) (1996a) *European Children's Literature I*, Kingston: Kingston University

Cotton, P. (1996b) *EPBC Teachers' Resource Book*, Kingston: Kingston University

Cotton, P. (1997) *The European Dimension in Picture Books*, unpublished PhD thesis, Durham University

Cotton, P. (ed) (1998) *European Children's Literature II*, Kingston: Kingston University

Cotton, P. (1999a) 'Picture Books: A European Perspective', in *Journal of Children's Literature*, Vol.25, No.1: 18-27, Spring 1999

Cotton, P. (1999b) 'The European Picture Book Collection', in *Children's Literature in Education*, Vol.30. No.2: 45-56, Autumn, 1999

Cotton, P. (2000) http://members.tripod.com/pennicotton

De Vries, A. (1996) 'Children's Literature in the Netherlands', in P. Hunt (ed.) *International Companion Encyclopedia of Children's Literature*, London: Routledge

Department for Education and Employment, (1998) *The National Literacy Strategy Framework for Teaching*, London: Stationery Office

Doonan, J. (1993) *Looking at Pictures in Picture Books*, Stroud: Thimble Press

Doonan, J. (1996) 'The modern picture book', in P. Hunt (ed.) *The International Companion Encyclopedia of Children's Literature*, London: Routledge

Dunbar, R. (1996) 'Children's Literature: The contemporary Irish dimension', in P. Cotton *European Children's Literature I*, Kingston: Kingston University

Dunn, O. (1995) *Help Your Child with a Foreign Language*, London: Hodder and Stoughton

Eco, U. (1981) *The Role of the Reader*, London: Hutchison

Eco, U. (1985) 'Producing signs' in M. Blonsky (ed.) *On Signs*, Baltimore: Johns Hopkins University Press

Ewers, H.H. (1996) 'Children's literature in Germany', in P. Hunt (ed.) *International Companion Encyclopedia of Children's Literature*, London: Routledge

Flugge, K. (1994) Unpublished group presentation at conference: *Introducing European Children's Books in Translation*, London: Roehampton Institute

Fox, G. (1996) ' Teaching ficton and poetry', in P. Hunt (ed.) *The International Companion Encyclopedia of Children's Literature*, London: Routledge

Gibbs, A. (1986) *Picture Books to Read Aloud,* London: Centre for Language in Primary Education

Glazer, J. and Williams G. (1979) *Introduction to Children's Literature*, New York: McGraw-Hill

Goodman P. (1954) *The Structure of Literature*, Chicago: University of Chicago Press

Graham, J. (1990) *Pictures on the Page*, Sheffield: NATE

Gregory, E. (1996) *Making Sense of a New World,* London: Paul Chapman

Hardy, B. (1977) 'Narrative as a Primary Act of Mind', in M. Meek, A. Warlow and G. Barton (eds.), *The Cool Web*, London: The Bodley Head

Hazard, P. (1932) *Les Livres, Les Enfants et Les Hommes*, Paris: Flammarion

Heap, J.L. (1985) 'Discourse in the production of classroom knowledge: reading lessons'. *Curriculum Inquiry*, Vol. 15: 245-79

Hodge, R. and Kress, G. (1988) *Social Semiotics*, Oxford: Polity Press

Hollindale, P. (1988) 'Ideology and the children's book', *Signal*, No. 55: 3-22

Hollindale, P. (1997) *Signs of Childness in Children's Books*, Stroud, Glos.: Thimble

Hunt, P. (ed.) (1996) *The International Companion Encyclopedia of Children's Literature*, London: Routledge

Hürlimann, B. (1967) *Three Centuries of Children's Books in Europe*, London: Oxford University Press

Iser, W.(1978) *The Act of Reading*, London: Routledge and Kegan Paul

Jobe, R. (1996) 'Translation', in P. Hunt (ed.) *The International Companion Encyclopedia of Children's Literature*, London: Routledge

Keiffer, B. (1995) *The Potential of Picture: From Visual Literacy to Aesthetic Understanding*, Englewood Cliffs, New Jersey: Prentice Hall, Inc.

Kerrigan, M. (1993) 'Words Lost in a New Landscape' in *Times Higher Educational Supplement*, 2nd April, 1993

Klein, G. (1985) *Reading into Racism: bias in children's literature and learning materials*, London: Routledge and Kegan Paul

Knudsen Lindauer, (1988) S.L. 'Wordless Books: An approach to Visual Literacy', *Children's Literature in Education*, Vol. 19, No. 3: 136-142

Kress, G. and van Leeuwen T. (1990) *Reading Images*, Victoria: Deakin University Press

Kreyder, L. (1996) 'Children's Literature in Italy', in P. Hunt (ed.) *International Companion Encyclopedia of Children's Literature*, London: Routledge

Lamb, M. (1997) *Europe Today*, Brussels: European Commission

Lewis, D. H. (1990) 'The constructedness of texts: picture books and the metafictive'. *Signal*: No. 62: 131-46

Lewis, D.H. (1994) *The Metafictive in Picture Books: A Theoretical Analysis of the Nature and Origins of Contemporary Children's Picture Books, with Case Studies of Children Reading Picture Book Texts*, Unpublished PhD. thesis, Institute of Education, London University

Lewis, D. H. (1996) 'Getting a grip on the picture book', *UKALCL Newsletter*, No 4: 3-10, June 1996

Marriott, S. (1991) *Picture Books in the Primary Classroom,* London: Paul Chapman

McCallum, R. (1996) 'Metafiction and experimental work', in P. Hunt (ed.) *The International Companion Encyclopedia of Children's Literature*, London: Routledge

Meek, M. (1988) *How Texts Teach What Readers Learn*, Stroud: Thimble Press

Meek, M. (1991) *On Being Literate*, London: The Bodley Head

Meek, M. (1996) 'Introduction', in P. Hunt (ed.) *International Companion Encyclopedia of Children's Literature*, London: Routledge

Metz, C. (1982) *The Imaginary Simplifier: Psychoanalysis and the Cinema*, Bloomington: Indiana University Press

Mitchell, W.J.T. (1986) *Iconology: Image, Text and Ideology*, Chicago: University of Chicago Press

Moebius, W. (1986) 'Introduction to Picture Book Codes', in *Word and Image*, Vol. 2: 141-51

Moss, E. (1981) *Picture Books for Young People 9-13*, South Woodchester: Signal

Moss, E. (1990) 'A certain particularity: an interview with Janet and Alan Ahlberg', *Signal 61*, 20-42, January, 1990

National Oracy Project, (1991) *Teaching, Talking and learning in Key Stage Two*, Sheffield: NATE.

National Writing Project, (1988) *Audiences for Writing*, Walton-on-Thames: Thomas Nelson.

Nières, I. (1992) 'Une Europe des livres de l'enfance', in Catalogue de l'exposition *Livres d'enfants en Europe*, France: Pontivy

Nodelman, P. (1988) *Words about Pictures: The Narrative Art of Children's Picture Books*, Athens Georgia, University of Georgia Press

Nodelman, P. (1996) 'Illustration and picture books', in P. Hunt (ed.) *International Companion Encyclopedia of Children's Literature,* London: Routledge

O'Sullivan, E. (1992) 'Does Pinocchio have an Italian passport? What is specifically National and what is International about classics of children's literature', in M.F. von Weizsäcker *The World of Children in Children's Books – Children's Books in the World of Children*, Munich: Iris-Druck, Karl Singer

Ogden, E. (1994) 'Intellectual and Physical Mobility in Higher Education in General and in Teacher Education in Particular' in S. Janssen and R. Loly-Smets (eds.) *RIF Symposium*, 1993, Brussels: European Commission

Oittinen R. (1991) 'On the situation of translation for the child: the dialogue between text and illustration', *USBBY Newsletter*, Vol. 16, 1: 13-18

Olmert, M. (1992) *The Smithsonian Book of Books*, Washington DC: Smithsonian Institute

Perkins, V. (1972) *Film as Film*, Harmondsworth: Penguin

Pierce, C. S. (1931) *Collected Papers*, Cambridge: Harvard University Press

Perrot, J. (1996a) 'Children's Literature in France', in P. Hunt (ed.) *International Companion Encyclopedia of Children's Literature*, London: Routledge

Perrot, J. (1996b) ' French pop-up books as a new cultural paradise for blissful budding child readers' in P. Cotton (ed.) *European Children's Literature*, Kingston: Kingston Universiy Press

Pinsent, P. (1997) *Children's Literature and the Politics of Equality*, Lomdon: David Fulton.

Pullman, P. (1989) 'Invisible pictures', *Signal 60*:160-166, September, 1989

Rocha, N. (1996) 'Children's Literature in Portugal', in P. Hunt (ed.) *International Companion Encyclopedia of Children's Literature*, London: Routledge

Rutschmann, V. (1996) 'Children's Literature in Switzerland', in P. Hunt (ed.) *International Companion Encyclopedia of Children's Literature*, London: Routledge

Satzke K. and Wolf, W. (1993) *Lehrplan der Volkschule*, Wein: OBV, Padagogischer Verlag

Saunders, Kathy (2000) *Happy Ever Afters: a storybook guide to teaching children about disability*, Stoke on Trent: Trentham

Saussure, F. D. (1916) *Cours Linguistique Générale*, Paris: Payot

Sendak, M. (1988) *Caldecott and Co,* London: Rhinehardt

Shulcvitz, U. (1985) *Writing with Pictures: How to Write and Illustrate Children's Books*, New York: Watson Gupthill

Surrallés, C.G., Verdulla, A.M. and Dorao, M. (1996) 'Children's Literature in Spain', in P. Hunt (ed.) *International Companion Encyclopedia of Children's Literature*, London: Routledge

Thomas, A. (1994) *The Illustrated Dictionary of Narrative Painting*, London: John Murray in association with the National Gallery

Velders, T. (1992) *Reading Images: Approaches to Visual Literacy*, Deventer: Rijkshogeschool Ijselland

Wallen, M. (1990) *Every Picture Tells...*, Sheffield: National Association for the Teaching of English

Watkins, T. (1992) 'Cultural studies, new historicism, and children's literature', in Hunt P. (ed.) *Literature for Children: Contemporary Criticism*, London: Routledge

Watson, V. and Styles M. (1996) *Talking Pictures*, London: Hodder and Stoughton

Wells, G. (1985) *Language, Learning and Education*, Walton on Thames: NFER, Nelson

Westin, B. (1991) *Children's Literature in Sweden*, Uddevalla: Bohusläningens Boktryckeri AB

Westin, B. (1996) 'Children's Literature in the Nordic countries', in P. Hunt (ed.) *International Companion Encyclopedia of Children's Literature*, London: Routledge

Wilkie, C. (1996) 'Intertextuality' in P. Hunt (ed.) *International Companion Encyclopedia of Children's Literature*, London: Routledge

Williams, M.L. (1996) 'Children's Literature in Wales', in P. Hunt (ed.) *International Companion Encyclopedia of Children's Literature*, London: Routledge

EPBC BIBLIOGRAPHY

Ahlberg, A.and J. (1990) *Starting School*, Middlesex, England: Picture Puffin

Baeten, L. (1996) *Lotje is jarig,* Hasselt, Belgium: Uitgeverij Clavis

Buisman, J. (1976) *Kees en Keetje*, Amsterdam, Netherlands: De Harmonie

Carpi, P. (1996) *La bambina che non voleva andare a dormire,* Trieste, Italy: Edizioni E.Elle

Foreman, M. (1978) *War and Peas*, Middlesex, England: Picture Puffin.

Gisbert, J.M. and Ruano A. (1990) *El guardián del olvido,* Madrid, Spain: Ediciones SM.

Hedderwick, M. (1993) *Katie Morag and the new pier*, London, England: Red Fox.

Jansson, T. (1984) *VEM ska trösta knyttet?* Finland: Jakobstads Tryckeri Och Tidnings AB

Kalow, G. and Bröger, A. (1966) *Hallo, kleiner Wal*, Stuttgart, Germany: Thiencmann

Kyritsopoulus, A. (1985) *The story-spinner meets the sugar-wizard*, Athens, Greece: Kedros

Lewis, S. and Morris, J. (1996) *Cantre'r Gwaelod*, Ceredigion, Wales: Argraffwyd gan Wasg Gomer, Llandysul

Malaquias, C. (1988) *A ovelha negra,* Lisbon: Portugal: Texto Editora

Nève, A. and Crowther, K. (1995) *Un jour mon Prince viendra*, Bruxelles, Belgium: L'école des loisirs

Olsen, I.S. (1994) *Mosekonens Bryg*, Vaerløse, Denmark: Gyldendal, Trykt Hos Grafodan Offset

Pommaux, Y. (1994) *Une nuit, un chat...*, Paris, France: L'école des loisirs

Rosenstock, G. (1995) *Naomh Pádraig agus Crom Dubh*, Dublin, Ireland: An Gúm

Stark, U. and Höglund, A. (1992) *Kan du vissla Johanna,* Stockholm, Sweden: Bonniers Juniorförlag

Theis, A. and Ries, M. (1995) *D'Grisette an D'Choupette um motorrad*, Luxembourg: Joseph Beffort

Ulitzka, I. and Gepp, G. (1993) *Das Land der Ecken*, Vienna, Austria: Picus

141

INDEX